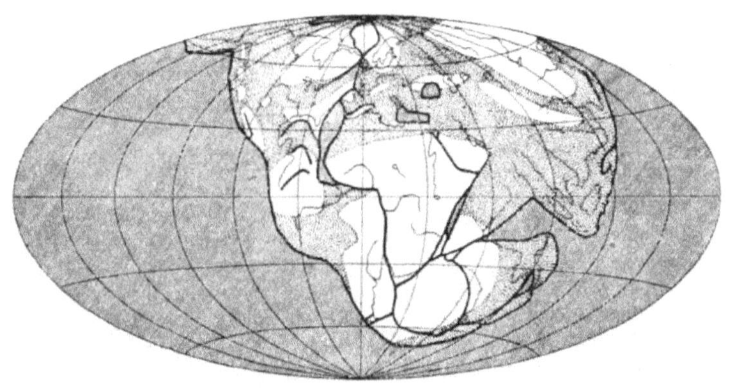

A Path to Oblivion

Survivor's Memoirs

written by Anthony Stevens

The ongoing environmental degradation, if left unaddressed, could set off a chain reaction of catastrophic events leading to a runaway collapse. This collapse would cause severe economic, social, and political shocks that would ripple through the interconnected global systems, surpassing our ability to manage them effectively. Unless we take immediate and significant action, we run the risk of repeating the fate of lemmings by blindly following a path that leads us into the abyss.

Grasses green fragrance
Harvests light from a distant star
Nourishing the Earth

Lying beneath -
A world tirelessly working
Giving life to all

The endless wonders -
Life's creators, never stopping
Wrapped in life's ribbon

Life is unstoppable
A circle of creators
Evermore evolving

Haiku

俳句

The Prologue

This is a fictional story about the lives of three generations of a family who are among the survivors of Earth's sixth mass extinction. Whilst the story is fictional, the possibility of extinction is very real. Should it happen it would not be the first time that most of Earth's life forms have disappeared, and been replaced long after by new life forms that evolved to meet the challenges of the new ecological landscape.

The story is a reflection on today's socio-economic standards and the injustices that exist for millions of people, and the reasons why world leaders are reluctant to go beyond their green rhetoric and hesitate in taking the steps to halt the path towards extinction.

Countless scientific research papers explain the changes and what will happen if ignored. One such paper, a UN report, says that farming practices, human behaviour and the world's economic system must change if we are to avoid extinction, and in a world driven by economic growth, these are extremely challenging goals as they deeply impact our everyday lives, making them difficult, and maybe impossible to implement.

Until now, the impacts of environmental change have been occurring at an increasing pace but have been largely manageable for high-income countries. They have been able to adapt to the floods, droughts and extreme temperatures and even accept them as a new norm, leaving them complacently believing that there is time to sort it out. In many low-income countries, their lack of financial resources and the necessary skills makes the situation very different. Droughts are increasing the likelihood of famine, and the constant extreme weather events such as floods and wildfires are creating food and freshwater shortages which are leaving millions of people homeless and starving, for them adaptation is not an option.

The list of changes to our world that are caused by anthropogenic activities is manifold. Ocean and land warming, shortages of fresh water, melting glaciers and ice-caps, CO_2 and methane gas released by melting tundra, loss of carbon sinks that sequester CO_2, wildfires releasing CO_2 and destroying biodiversity, extreme weather events, nitrogen compounds released by fossil fuels and farming creating air and water pollution and destroying biodiversity, microplastics and the ubiquitous use of forever chemicals present in all life forms, dwindling crop yields and fish stocks due to over farming, and loss of pollinators. These changes, together with the world's social and economic injustices, are what is threatening our very existence.

All of this is happening now and has been doing so for decades, and it is clear that the pace of change is accelerating. As each year passes we are left with less time to stop or reverse the changes, yet there are still those who struggle to accept the urgency of taking remedial actions.

Even when our political leaders have acknowledged the emergency by signing global agreements, individually they must allocate budgets and introduce changes to people's lives without losing their confidence. A major issue with global agreements on climate change is that they often require long-term planning and action, which can conflict with the short-term goals and priorities of political leaders who may only be in power for a few years. This can lead to a lack of sustained effort and funding towards meeting these goals, as future leaders may not be as committed or focused on them. Additionally, competing economic pressures can make it difficult to allocate budgets towards green initiatives, even when there is widespread recognition of their importance. The consequences of demure attitudes towards the environmental crisis can be disastrous, leading to further economic and social entropies.

Even today with so much evidence to say that we must act immediately to reduce carbon emissions, there are many industries, often major contributors to global warming, that employ various guises to block legislation that could harm their profits.

The complexities of the issues, and the consequences of inaction, are impossible to comprehend for most people. There is no reference point, nothing like this has ever happened before to the human race. Global pandemics have destroyed millions of lives over the centuries, but a catastrophe of this magnitude is not solved with a vaccine, it can only be stopped by changing the way we live.

Many of the measures that are needed to reduce the impact of climate breakdown involve making changes to the way we live. Some of the measures could impact what we eat, how we travel, and possibly many more, and may turn voters towards populist politics, believing that they can avoid imposing the changes and maintain life as normal. The nationalistic and libertine policies of these populist political parties and their unabashed mendacity can lead to a global permacrisis and disparate relationships, the opposite of what is needed.

Unchecked climate change could trigger the mass

migration of billions of people in search of food and water, which could exacerbate political and economic instability, ultimately leading to the rise of populist and nationalist movements. This, in turn, could result in economic protectionism and the breakdown of global supply chains, further compounding the problems caused by climate change. Such instability may also fuel the growth of extremist groups that seek to exploit the misfortunes of others. Moreover, the possibility of a global nuclear war cannot be discounted, and this could result in widespread devastation, further exacerbating efforts to address climate change.

Geopolitical, social, and geographic factors have hindered the world's collective efforts to address major climate goals. To overcome these obstacles, there is an urgent need for a global governing body with the mandate and authority to direct and enforce the necessary changes. However, the creation of such an organization is challenging to envision, as many countries currently prioritize nationalistic and religious beliefs over the notion of a global community. This dilemma is one that our leaders must face, as failure to act decisively could result in catastrophic consequences for our planet and its inhabitants.

Young people around the world are experiencing growing anxiety about their future, particularly in light of the failures of those in power to address critical issues such as climate change. Thanks to the courageous efforts of a teenage girl and a nonagenarian man, there has been a surge of youth activism across the globe, with increasing numbers of young people demanding urgent action and using unconventional tactics to make their voices heard. These activists recognize that the threat of a climate catastrophe is real and immediate and that without swift action, the future is uncertain. It is imperative that leaders around the world listen to these voices and take bold action to address the climate crisis.

While individual efforts to reduce carbon emissions are important, they alone are not sufficient to address the scale of the problem. Governments around the world must collaborate on a global scale to achieve the necessary changes. Many of the world's leading economies have made commitments to reduce carbon emissions, with some aiming for net-zero emissions by 2050 or even earlier. However, it remains to be seen whether these pledges will be sufficient to prevent the worst effects of climate change. Urgent and sustained action is needed to address this global crisis and secure a sustainable future for generations to come.

While efforts to reduce carbon emissions are important, they are only one piece of the puzzle when it comes to protecting the planet's ecosystems. There are many other factors contributing to the loss of biodiversity, shortages of food and fresh water, and pollution, all of which are catastrophic events that threaten our future. Additionally, the global economic system is plagued by inequality, and addressing this issue is crucial to ensuring a sustainable future for all. The G20 nations have a responsibility to reduce poverty and address the distribution of wealth, as well as assist countries suffering from the effects of climate change. Failure to do so could lead to mass migrations, terrorism, and armed conflicts, as we are already seeing in many regions around the world, including Europe and the United States. We must take action now to address these pressing issues and secure a sustainable future for generations to come.

Today's "throw-away" society demands low-cost, easily affordable products, which often leads retailers to apply downward economic pressures on the suppliers, who in turn, are compelled to pay low wages and provide poor working conditions. This system of wealth creation must somehow change, so that it doesn't thrive on low-cost labour and increase the number of consumers, thus driving population growth, and creating further pressures on the planet's finite resources.

The challenges of solving the problems are manifold. The global infrastructures for providing us with the way of life that we enjoy, involve complex networks of production facilities, supply chains and distribution channels. The number of people that they employ and the large investments involved, can not be changed without serious consequences to global economies and people's lives.

The huge quantities of investment capital that are available will always follow the most attractive profits, and unless the measures needed to solve the crises can quickly provide competitive investment opportunities, the capital investments that are required are unlikely to be forthcoming at a time when they are most needed.

Even if technological innovation succeeds in addressing the issues, the ecological and social issues that have led us to the point of extinction do not go away unless the corrective measures include a wide range of changes to the way we live, and that billions of people are prepared to adopt them. It is possible that the upward pressures on biodiversity, carbon emissions, and pollution, continue to increase in the wake of population growth, and when linked with the incongruity of wealth distribution, and the globally interwoven economies and supply networks, the possibility of a chaotic end to the human race remains real.

As I mentioned, the world of the future will have to function very differently than it does today to be able to support the continuance of mankind. If there is a rapid response to the major catastrophic events that the planet is experiencing today, it may save the majority of mankind, but it will lead to extreme changes in the way we live.

By taking proactive measures to mitigate the impacts of climate change, such as investing in renewable energy sources and promoting sustainable agriculture and forestry practices, we can reduce the likelihood of such catastrophic events. Additionally, we can work towards creating more resilient communities that can better cope with the effects of climate change, such as through improved infrastructure and disaster preparedness planning. By taking these steps, we can not only protect the environment but possibly safeguard our societies and economies from the worst impacts of climate change but only if these steps are applied to the vast majority of the world population.

A delayed response to the events will undoubtedly change the planet's ecology, the hope would be that enough would be done in time to halt the complete collapse of the Earth's ecosystems, and allow the recovery of flora and fauna, and with it, the survival of mankind. No response will undoubtedly lead to the extinction of homo sapiens.

My pessimism about our ability to react in time and avoid a cataclysm is reflected in this story, however, I do retain the hope that mankind can work together and avoid complete annihilation, but sadly, I fear that things must get much worse before they attract required corrective measures, by which time, it may be too late.

I shan't be around to witness if Mankind will succeed or fail. So with this catharsis story, I have imagined how the human race might survive an apocalyptic outcome. In it, I have assumed that technological advancements in the next 50 years will enable survivors to exist with unlimited electricity provided by nuclear fusion and that there will be a comprehensive data warehouse of knowledge. I've also assumed that the advancements in robotics will provide skilled and unskilled labour, and military defence systems will be almost undefeatable. I don't think that any of these assumptions are unrealistic.

The future of mankind lies in the hands of today's adolescents, they will be the ones voting for the leaders and forming the industrial and political leaders. It is for us to provide them with the appropriate knowledge and skills to undertake those crucial roles.

One thing is for certain, we must create a symbiotic relationship between the human race and the natural world.

Reflections

Can we solve the climate crisis?

The simple answer is yes. With the right global initiatives and the utilisation of technology, there is every hope that the catastrophic ravages of a changing world can be avoided or minimized.

However, the real questions are:

"Can our current leaders save us?"

"Can technology help to save us?"

The prologue explains why I believe that our current leaders are not able to solve the climate crisis, and what I think is needed to address that. Technologies such as geothermal, wind, solar, hydro and tidal power sources, with the right investment incentives, can reduce the continuance of carbon emissions and prevent further destruction to biodiversity, thus softening the impact by addressing mainly the symptoms, and not the major causes, which are the pressures on the Earth's natural resources and global inequality, thus leaving the omnipresence of extinction real.

One major technological innovation that can provide a long-term solution, is nuclear fusion. As yet unproven, its utilisation will unlikely be available in time to halt our downward path to extinction. Switching traditional industries that produce energy through burning fossil fuels to produce energy using these carbon-free alternatives will take time as it will impact their entire upstream and downstream platforms.

On the bright side, not too long ago a hole in the Earth's ozone layer was developing due to the use of chlorofluorocarbons (CFCs). This layer is essential for life to exist, its molecules act as a shield protecting us from solar radiation. Due to global cooperation, the use of these chemicals is being controlled and now the ozone hole is supposed to be closed within the next 20 years. Although the solution is far simpler than what is required to solve the environmental crisis, it does show that global cooperation is achievable and can make a difference.

Why are we complacent?

Even though climate deniers are now in the minority, our enthusiasm to take the facts of climate change seriously as what is needed is still inadequate. There are some people, sadly few, who see the importance of immediate action, but many, although acknowledging the threats, rarely take their actions beyond attempting to reduce their carbon footprint and reduce their levels of pollution, leaving others to solve the real issues. This catharsis attitude is often reflected in the behaviour of our leaders.

Complacency is a complex phenomenon that can have multiple underlying causes. In the case of climate change, there may be several reasons why people are complacent or not taking enough action.

One reason may be a lack of understanding of the urgency and severity of the problem. Climate change is a slow and gradual process, which can make it difficult for people to perceive its immediate impact. Additionally, people may not fully grasp the long-term consequences of inaction, such as the potential for irreparable damage to the planet's ecosystems.

Another reason for complacency may be a sense of powerlessness or apathy. Some people may feel overwhelmed by the scale of the problem or believe that their individual actions cannot make a significant difference. Others may feel disillusioned or cynical about the ability of governments and other institutions to effect real change.

Finally, there may be economic or political factors that discourage action on climate change. Some individuals or corporations may prioritize short-term profits over long-term sustainability, while politicians may be hesitant to take bold action for fear of losing public support or upsetting powerful interest groups.

Addressing complacency will likely require a multifaceted approach, including education and outreach efforts to increase awareness of the severity of the problem and the potential for individual action, as well as policy changes that incentivize sustainable behaviour and penalize unsustainable practices. It will also require a shift in societal attitudes toward greater recognition of the importance of environmental stewardship and the need to take action to ensure a sustainable future.

Just a thought

Dinosaurs existed for 165 million years without ever developing the type of intelligence that we have. This it could be argued is what enabled their longevity as the use of our intelligence has altered our environment through our anthropogenic activities and has put us on this path towards the possibility of extinction. I have often wondered who would be the apex predator today had the asteroid that decimated the dinosaurs missed the Earth.

I would hypothesize that it would still be Tyrannosaurus Rex or some evolved version of it. Of course, changing environmental conditions or competition from other species could have led to the decline or extinction of certain dinosaur groups.

Ultimately, speculating about what might have happened in an alternate timeline is a fun-thought experiment, evolution and ecological dynamics are complex and unpredictable as many factors can influence the survival and success of a species, making it impossible to say with certainty how things would have played out if the asteroid had missed the Earth other than to say it would have been very different.

Chapter One

First Generation

My name is Jarvid Guta, I am a ninety-five-year-old somewhat feeble widower. This is my story of the horrific events that led to the life that I am leading today.

The year is 2122, and I have been incarcerated in a living tomb for forty-seven years. My very existence depends on artificiality, the air, the food, the climate, and even the light, nothing in my world is natural. I am living the life of a troglodyte.

I grew up in a high-rise apartment in Singapore. Advic, my father, was a third-generation Indian, and my mother, Ella, was also descended from a migrant family who moved from China four generations ago. They instilled in me a love of learning and a drive to excel. As I grew older, my passion for microbiology emerged, and I pursued it with fervour, eventually earning a first-class honours degree in the field.

To celebrate my 23rd birthday, my parents generously funded my pursuit of a Bachelor of Science degree in Microbiology from the esteemed

University of Malaya in Kuala Lumpur. With their unwavering emotional and financial support, I completed my studies and graduated with distinctions. Upon my return to Singapore, I received a graduate study grant from the government to pursue a Master's degree in Microbiology at Princeton University. Despite their sadness at my departure, my parents remained selfless in their support of my aspirations, and for that, I am forever grateful.

Following a year of dedicated study in the United States, I resolved to broaden my horizons and socialize more. It was at a campus party that I first met Lucy, an American microbiology student from the Midwest who was a year behind me in school and a year younger. As we got to know each other, we discovered a shared affinity for many things, and several months later, we took the leap and moved into a furnished apartment just off-campus. Our relationship blossomed and strengthened, and I knew that I had found someone truly special.

Our first year together was a wonderful adventure. We both dedicated ourselves to completing our studies while discovering our mutual love for a diverse range of cultural interests. As our relationship continued to blossom, we knew that we wanted to spend the rest of our lives together. So, in 2052, we decided to formalize our commitment by getting married, much to the delight of our parents. The wedding ceremony was a quiet civil affair held in Lucy's hometown, attended by both sets of parents. Given our different cultural and religious backgrounds, we opted for a secular ceremony that was simple and elegant. Happily, our parents didn't have any objections to our choice of ceremony, as they didn't practice any particular religion.

We broached the topic of starting a family before completing our studies with our parents, and at first, they were hesitant, insisting that our education should come first. However, once we explained that we wanted to relish our time with our children while we were still young and healthy, and give our future grandchildren even more years to enjoy with us, they began to see things from our perspective. Thankfully, they agreed to continue providing us with their unwavering emotional and financial support.

In 2053, we welcomed our healthy twins, Henry and Cleo, into the world. Though they weren't identical, they shared many physical and mental similarities that only strengthened their bond. Naturally, our lives became more challenging with the arrival of our little ones, but we remained focused on completing our studies. In 2054, Lucy earned her Master's degree, and the previous year, I earned mine. In 2058, I was thrilled to receive my

PhD, and once again, a year later, Lucy earned hers. Through hard work and dedication, we managed to balance our academic pursuits with our responsibilities as new parents.

As our twins grew more active and curious, we found that parenting became increasingly demanding. We realized that advancing our careers simultaneously would be challenging, so we decided to pursue research and development projects in an academic setting. This not only allowed us to spend more time with our children but also allowed us to pursue something we were passionate about. Most importantly, we felt that we were making a meaningful contribution to the world, given the challenges our society was facing.

In 2059, we eagerly applied for positions advertised by Ghent University in Belgium. The university was seeking two experts to lead government-funded projects in Microbiology, an area of science that perfectly matched our qualifications and interests. We were thrilled when we learned that we had both been accepted for the positions. Our research projects aimed to deepen our understanding of microorganisms and their interactions with their environments, with the ultimate goal of improving human health. We looked forward to studying how microorganisms grow and develop, and how we can harness their properties for the benefit of society.

Despite our initial concerns about adapting to a new culture, language, and way of life, we eagerly set out for Belgium in the early spring of 2060, ready to begin our new journey at Ghent University. We were delighted to find that our worries were completely unfounded. From the moment we arrived, we were welcomed with open arms and settled into a beautiful old house in the heart of Ghent, with ample space for both work and leisure. Although we found that many people in Ghent spoke English, we recognized the value of learning Dutch and French to better communicate with those outside of our academic circle. We enrolled in language courses and soon found ourselves conversing confidently with locals, immersing ourselves in the rich culture and history of this vibrant city.

We decided to enrol our five-year-old twins in a local school, recognizing the value of immersing them in the local culture and language. We were pleased to see that our decision paid off, as they adapted quickly to their new environment, made friends with Belgian children, and eagerly embraced their studies. It was heartwarming to see how easily they navigated the transition and became comfortable in their new surroundings. We were proud of their resilience and openness to new experiences and knew that this would serve them well in their future endeavours.

Lucy was entrusted with leading a critical research project aimed at finding treatments for a highly infectious outbreak of the NIPAH virus. This virus, a distant cousin of the measles virus, has the potential to cause significant harm, with a mortality rate of up to 75% among infected individuals. It poses a serious threat to public health, as it can be transmitted to humans through close contact with infected pigs, as well as by consuming raw food contaminated with urine or saliva from infected bats. The urgent need for effective treatments and preventative measures cannot be overstated, given the potential for the NIPAH virus to trigger a devastating global pandemic. With Lucy at the helm of this vital research, there was hope for a brighter, healthier future for all.

Under Lucy's leadership, her team made groundbreaking strides in the development of Monoclonal antibodies for the treatment of viral infections. Not only were they successful in developing Monoclonal antibodies for the NIPAH virus, but they also devised innovative procedures for creating and testing Monoclonal antibodies for other viral strains. Their approach eliminated the need to obtain existing antibodies, enabling laboratories to simulate the structure of any known virus and create a single cell for the development of a Monoclonal antibody and level-one testing. This technology paved the way for the creation of a digital bank of partially tested and approved vaccines, ready for rapid approvals and distribution in response to new viral infections.

In recognition of her extraordinary work, Lucy was awarded the Nobel Prize for Medicine in 2064 for her groundbreaking contributions to the field of 'gain-of-function' research. Her collaboration with fellow researchers resulted in the design of new technology that has revolutionized the field and has the potential to save countless lives in the future. Her dedication to advancing science and improving global health served as an inspiration to us all.

While my contributions may have been less widely recognized, my work was no less important in the battle against viruses. I was entrusted with leading a team tasked with researching innovative methods to instruct the immune system in recognizing and neutralizing viral infections. Although our successes may not have resulted in a Nobel Prize, we were proud of the progress we made in developing new strategies for combating a wide range of viral diseases. By working in tandem with Lucy's team, we were able to make significant strides towards the goal of improving global health and mitigating the threat of viral pandemics. Even small steps forward in this critical field can make a world of difference, and I am honoured to have played a role in this important work.

While life in Belgium offered us both pleasure and security, and we relished the academic challenges of our work, we couldn't help but be conscious of the stark contrast between our experience and the struggles faced by millions of people in conflict-ridden parts of the world. Despite our contentment, we felt a deep sense of empathy for those who were not as fortunate as we were.

The Realisation

Climate change has been impacting people's lives for many years, and the effects became more noticeable since 2020. In light of this, Lucy and I made significant changes to our lifestyle. We adopted a vegan diet to lower our carbon footprint and did our best to recycle everything we could and avoided using plastics. We also made a conscious effort to wear environmentally friendly clothing. While we knew that many people in wealthier countries shared our commitment to sustainability, we recognized that not everyone could or wanted to participate. Unfortunately, some people preferred to ignore the issue altogether, rather than face the hard truths of the changing climate.

Despite the high cost of living that left little room for recreation, my partner and I still managed to take vacations to escape the unbearable summer heat. While many people headed to coastal areas, we preferred to drive to cooler regions such as Scandinavia or the Alps, where we could camp and enjoy nature. Our old home, like most homes in the developed world, was equipped with air conditioning and insulation to keep us cool during the hot months. We recognized our privilege and felt fortunate to have access to such resources.

However, we also acknowledged that millions of people, particularly those living in poorer countries, lacked such basic amenities and were at risk of life-threatening temperatures.

Despite a growing number of couples electing to have one or no children, the decline in men's sperm count and armed conflicts resulting in the loss of millions of lives, the world's population continued to rise rapidly. In just over two decades since the start of the millennium, the population surged by three billion to reach a staggering nine billion.

As the population continued to grow, so did the demand for resources in both developed and developing countries. This increase in demand put immense pressure on resources and exacerbated existing difficulties. Cities, already overcrowded due to the millions displaced by rising sea levels, became even more congested. Additionally, food and property prices soared, and crowded conditions were pervasive everywhere one looked. The increase in demand for resources impacted everyone, and solutions were needed to address these pressing issues.

Significant progress had been made in the industry's transition to green energy, with substantial investments in green technologies. The objective of achieving carbon neutrality by 2050 had been largely attained, with some countries even meeting it by 2030. Although this was an optimistic development, it only applied to a few leading industrialized countries and not all. Achieving carbon neutrality levels meant that the amount of carbon dioxide released into the atmosphere was equal to the amount removed from it. However, this alone was inadequate to offset the escalating carbon dioxide and methane emissions from melting arctic and ocean tundra. Additionally, it did not account for the loss of natural carbon dioxide extraction processes, which were previously provided by the forest, bogs, oceans and soil.

For more than thirty years, catastrophic events have been occurring in various forms and with increasing frequency. The debate regarding the prevention of further escalation in global temperatures had become more widespread and intense. By 2050, the global temperature had increased by 2.3°C. It was now evident that concerted global efforts were required to ensure that the increase does not exceed 3.0°C, and everything possible must be done to prevent it from happening.

The International Organization of Climate Commitment (IOCC) was established in 2035 to replace the Conference of the Parties (COP) in addressing global environmental issues. Despite being a global body representing the Earth, it encountered difficulties in convincing world leaders to take decisive action to prevent further environmental damage. Although leaders met regularly to discuss critical proposals for urgent action, the IOCC struggled to gain their support. Some proposals were rejected, while others were watered down, even though leaders were well aware that this was their final opportunity to prevent an environmental catastrophe. Despite their commitments and pledges, world leaders' primary focus remained on pleasing their electorates, with budgets being directed towards economic issues often caused by climate change or seeking economic and political advantages over others. Unfortunately, profits still took precedence, despite the undeniable threat of environmental disaster.

At this moment, the flaws in human behaviour played a significant and detrimental role in the events that followed. Although the majority of electorates recognized the importance and urgency of addressing climate change, those in wealthier nations who had the means to mitigate the effects of climatic events became increasingly complacent. This complacency led many to believe that science could overcome any environmental threat, and that life could continue as normal. I too shared this belief, thinking that technology held all the answers, but it was only partly true. While those of us in prosperous regions of the world could live with the impacts of climate change, billions of people struggled to find food and water, which posed an existential threat to humanity. We were insulated from the worst effects of climate change, but many others were not.

The most daunting challenge was persuading leaders of wealthy nations to help save the lives of those struggling to survive, who had little input or interest in preventing climate change. At the time, it was argued that it was too late to assist them, and reversing the effects of climate change on their lives was no longer feasible. Although large sums of money were invested in their economies, these funds had a little long-term impact on their daily lives.

Then Came The Floods

In 2064, our lives took a turn for the worse when one of the most devastating impacts of climate change struck Belgium. The Flanders polders had been experiencing flooding for centuries, and some areas around the river Meuse had been dealing with floods for several decades. The most recent major flood occurred in 1953 when the lowlands were flooded due to the severest storm surge ever recorded in this part of the North Sea. This was compounded by three consecutive high spring tides that claimed the lives of thousands of people.

Due to the persistent threat of global warming, the low countries reinforced their sea defences, which had been under attack from rising sea levels and water seeping up through the ground for several years. Despite these efforts, the defences could not withstand the onslaught of a severe storm and an exceptionally high tide, resulting in flooding in the estuarial towns of The Netherlands and large parts of northern Flanders. The cities of Ghent and most of Flanders were left vulnerable to the risk of flooding, prompting urgent action to protect the ancient cities of Antwerp, Brugge, and Ghent. However, at the time, I was sceptical of the feasibility of these efforts, and as events unfolded, my doubts were unfortunately proven right.

The whole of the lowlands eventually succumbed to the ocean, including all of the beautiful cities and the thousands of years of history that they imbued.

The members and facilities of our University relocated entirely to the historic city of Louvain, which sat 25 meters above sea level, having lost 1.5 meters due to climate change. Upon arrival, we easily adapted to our new surroundings, settling into a spacious apartment in a newly built facility located close to the city. Our twins, who were already fluent in Dutch, found the transition to Louvain, another Dutch-speaking commune, effortless. Our lives were comfortable, and we enjoyed our work, but we were acutely aware that this sense of security might be short-lived.

Europe had been experiencing frequent violent storms with winds reaching 170-220 kph, battering coastal areas and creating sea level surges of 2 to 3 meters. Our winters had intensified, and unbearably hot summers caused untold damage to crops all over Europe. Life was becoming more intolerable for us, but for millions of people living without electricity, water, and food, it was much worse. This led to conflicts in all corners of the globe, as authoritarian regimes and paramilitary groups claiming to represent the frustrations and desperation of the masses began to emerge.

In the rapidly changing global landscape, many people were optimistic that technology held all the solutions. However, the surrender of the lowlands to the rising sea levels was clear evidence of mankind's vulnerability and the urgent need for action. We recognized that the speed at which these changes were occurring meant that without swift and drastic measures, there was a high probability that our children would be the last generation of Homo sapiens.

Clinging To Straws

The world had been in a state of turmoil for several decades, with the impacts of climate change being felt in every corner of the planet. Unfortunately, this only served to exacerbate the situation as the pressures of climate change drove people towards populist political parties that made empty promises and lacked the competence to address the issue. As a result, efforts to combat climate change were hindered, and it wasn't until it was too late that people realized the inadequacy of populist politics. Replacing the damage done to international agreements and re-establishing a globally balanced economy would take a long time.

It is astonishing that even in the face of a global crisis, efforts to save the world were still being hindered by the overriding need for profit-making, politicians who prioritized pleasing their electorates, and autocratic leaders who were focused solely on maintaining their power. Most people acknowledged the importance of solving climate change, but only if it does not significantly affect their daily lives. The world was in such chaos that the majority of the global population rose against their discredited leaders, both elected and autocratic. This forced leaders to acknowledge the urgent need to address issues at a global level.

In 2065, the IOCC was replaced by a new organization called the "World Climate Organization." This supranational organization required member countries to cede authority and sovereignty on climate, biodiversity, pollution, and geopolitical matters, and its decisions were binding on its members. The world's leaders mandated the organization to unilaterally compel coordinated action to prevent further environmental damage and prepare a plan to save humanity from the possibility of mass extinction. This initiative was long overdue and came very late in the worsening environmental changes.

The WCO faced an insurmountable hurdle in convincing the world's wealthiest countries, whose own economies were under tremendous pressure, that they must address the inequalities created by the global economic system and share their wealth with impoverished nations. Climate change was having an even greater impact on the economies of these nations, leading to a rapid decline in their little wealth. This process of impoverishment was affecting approximately two-thirds of the world's population, or to put it another way, six billion people.

Then, the WCO received the much-needed financial backing to provide technical and economic support for countries to improve their food production methods, revive their biospheres and natural habitats, and prevent further loss of biodiversity. Finally, the world was coming together to tackle the issue of preventing the Earth's temperature from rising by 4.0°C by the end of the century.

However, if the current economic model was not reformed, it would inevitably lead humanity towards an act of self-destruction. The growing number of impoverished people posed an increasing threat to others, and saving the planet was not even a consideration for them. While they had little to offer, their actions added to the already tangled web of the devastation caused by climate change.

Some wealthier countries struggled to make significant changes to their economies to address climate change. While the WCO was created to take on the responsibility of coordinating global action, it faced challenges in delivering aid to struggling countries. Corruption was a significant issue in some areas, and aid funds were not always used effectively to create a sustainable future for those in need.

In reality, even with the support provided by the WCO, there was little that could be done within the time left to solve their problems. The support they received took time to install as they not only lacked the financial resources, but they also lacked the technology, the skills, and the infrastructure. What irony! The wealthy countries were responsible for climate change, but it was the countries that had been producing relatively low emissions over the centuries that were mainly impacted by the changes.

Despite the global disruptions, we felt slightly optimistic about the future, as humanity had finally taken globally coordinated steps to avoid ecological disaster. However, some scientists claimed that we had already surpassed many tipping points, and there was no turning back. Ecological destruction is a gradual process, and many of the destructive processes had already become well-established. But we believed, or maybe hoped, that we could still avoid the worst.

As virologists, our work had become increasingly important due to the emergence of viral epidemics around the world. In the 21st century, three pandemics of highly infectious novel viruses had brought the world to a standstill. Thankfully, Lucy's research had been life-saving, as she had developed a method for the rapid development and approval of vaccines within just three months. However, despite this progress, the impact of these epidemics on people's lives and economies remained significant, and they were also negatively impacting efforts to fund environmental initiatives.

False Victories

By 2070 the world's largest economies and polluters had by now achieved net zero, or in some cases zero carbon emissions, largely by the use of green energies and other carbon reduction initiatives. This was further improved by the introduction of nuclear fusion reactors that first appeared in 2072, and quickly spread throughout the world thanks to WCO funding.

Despite the progress made in the fight against climate change, the release of carbon dioxide and methane gasses from sources such as surface and marine tundras continued to be a significant problem. Moreover, the loss of natural carbon sinks was still a concern. To address these issues, new technologies such as agrivoltaics, which combine solar energy production with agriculture, were extensively deployed. However, due to the magnitude of the problem, the results were unable to meet the demands. Similarly, an initiative to re-ice the Arctic regions by creating cloud coverage during the summer months had proved to be feasible. Still, replacing the billions of tonnes of ice lost over the decades was too great a task. It would take hundreds, if not thousands, of years to accomplish.

Long overdue global initiatives to reintroduce some natural carbon sinks such as planting vast areas of forests and mangroves, growing seagrass and kelp fields, and rewilding vast areas of arable land, were successful but once more, the scale of the challenge and the continuing threats from extreme climate events and the warming oceans, meant it would take decades to rebalance the Earth's ecosystems.

The importance of these initiatives was clear to Lucy and me, but we were becoming increasingly disillusioned and fearful for the future of our children. Like millions of others, we understood the urgency and importance of taking action to control climate change. However, time was running out, and we couldn't help but feel frustrated with our predecessors who had wasted decades before taking adequate measures. Scientists had warned that passing a tipping point would make it impossible to reverse the effects of climate change.

Like many millions of others, we devoted a significant part of our lives to supporting lobbying groups and attending climate change forums. Our lives were almost completely consumed by what was happening around us. Despite all of our efforts, we felt defeated. We believed there was nothing else we could do to prevent the world from reaching a final tipping point, and we didn't know what else could be done at this late stage. We held onto the possibility that new technologies might save the planet from a total extinction event.

People had grown tired of hearing repeated warnings of extinction, leading to complacency and feelings of resignation and the idea that extinction was inevitable.

The Precipice

The realisation of the predictions that by the end of the 21st century, life on Earth would become unsustainable for humanity seemed inevitable, as the global temperature had already risen by 3.0°C despite enormous efforts to prevent it. One of the consequences of the higher temperature was to accelerate the rate of warming, it was now predicted to reach 4.0°C within a decade, further exacerbating the already dire situation.

We, like many others, were aware of what needed to be done. It had been common knowledge for decades that we had to change the global economic model, control population growth, and live more simply while wasting less. However, these aspirations were still being opposed, as they were deemed detrimental to economies and necessitated vast changes in people's lives. People in high-polluting countries continued to live their lives as normally as possible while they still had the chance. Wealthy individuals built life-supporting structures to protect themselves and their families from the impacts of an environmental catastrophe.

At the 2073 meeting of the WCO, world leaders finally acknowledged the unavoidable path toward extinction that humanity was on. It was agreed that the focus would now shift to minimizing the impact and salvaging what was left of the ecology and saving the human race, as tipping points had already been breached.

At that crucial meeting, the WCO was given the mandate to enforce significant changes by imposing heavy financial penalties and even undertaking military interventions in extreme situations. These enforcement measures were applied to every country and backed up by the UN, NATO, and the military forces of major powers. The urgency was no longer a question, and there were no more equivocations, delays, or denials. The survival of the entire human race was at stake, and action needed to be taken immediately.

We learnt later that the WCO had been given another mandate to secure the survival of the human race in the event of a catastrophic collapse of the Earth's ecosystem. Under the utmost secrecy, they gathered a group of scientists and asked them to come up with a solution that would save the human race from extinction. They were given carte blanche and told that their solution must be multiracial and can not be affiliated with any religion, race or society. If approved, it would be adopted globally and enforced through coercive measures. All decisions had to be based on science and could not be politically influenced.

Knowing that the planet's ecosystems would eventually recover from the brink of extinction, the challenge for the WCO was to expedite the recovery process and ensure the survival of the human race until that day arrived. It was a daunting task, for they knew that minimizing the damage to the environment would require implementing harsh and disruptive changes that would likely result in the loss of billions of lives.

What Next?

As we entered the new decade, it became increasingly clear that the world was facing significant challenges. Many parts of the world were grappling with political instability, economic inequality, and environmental degradation. In some regions, authoritarian regimes had gained power and were imposing harsh restrictions on civil liberties and human rights. Meanwhile, the global population continued to grow, putting tremendous strain on resources such as food and water.

One of the most pressing issues we observed was the rapid spread of infectious diseases, which often disproportionately affected vulnerable populations. Mass migrations of people, driven by factors such as war, famine, and climate change, created conditions that facilitated the spread of pathogens. Our research aimed to understand the mechanisms behind these disease outbreaks and develop strategies to mitigate their impact. We recognized that these efforts were only a small part of the larger picture, but we remained committed to contributing to solutions that could help make the world a safer and healthier place for all.

Lucy and I sat down to discuss our future. I held onto hope that world leaders would take action in time to save some of the human race from the impending environmental collapse. However, Lucy had a different perspective; she believed that it was too late and that no amount of intervention could prevent the collapse of the planet's ecosystem. She argued that too many changes had already occurred and that we were past the point of no return.

While I believed that technology could help us minimize the impact of our anthropogenic activities, Lucy's view was that the problem went much deeper. The inhospitable climatic conditions were just the tip of the iceberg. The world's economies and global supply infrastructures were disrupted by geo-political obstacles caused by governments' insular attitudes towards retaining resources for themselves.

As we weighed the pros and cons of our different views, we both realised that the situation was complex and multifaceted. It was not just a problem for those directly affected by the changing climate but a global issue that required collaboration and cooperation at all levels. Despite our disagreements, we both agreed that we needed to do our part in contributing to solutions that could mitigate the impact of climate change and pave the way for a more sustainable future.

Lucy and I were both concerned about the future and agreed that we needed to consider how we could secure our survival in case things went wrong. We initially thought about moving to a remote place where the worst changes may not reach, but we soon realized that this was not a viable solution. We knew that such places would become overwhelmed by masses of people, leading to a dystopian and dangerous environment.

We also heard about wealthy families and business enterprises constructing large enclosures in an attempt to create a survival environment. However, we quickly dismissed this idea as we lacked the resources to buy into such solutions. Furthermore, we believed that isolation could cause significant stress and threaten the sustainability of such enclosures. Violence from the surrounding dystopian environment could also pose a significant threat.

Despite our concerns, we did not have a solution. We recognized that the challenges facing us and the world were complex and required collective action. As individuals, we felt that the best we could do was to stay informed, keep an open mind, and continue to contribute positively to society. We knew that we could not solve the problem alone, but we remained hopeful that together, we could work towards a better future.

In 2076, our lives took a dramatic turn after we received a letter from the WCO. The letter invited us to an interview in Geneva for a research project aimed at securing the survival of the human race. The letter did not specify the purpose of the meetings, but we were informed that we would need to speak to three committees over two days. Along with the letter, we received a form that we had to sign and return immediately, agreeing not to disclose any information regarding the letter or the meetings to anyone.

Our parents kindly offered to look after our twins while we accepted the invitation and boarded a train to Geneva. Upon arrival, we were greeted and driven to a hotel close to the WCO headquarters. The next day, we were escorted to a spacious room within the WCO building.

We sat before three sociologists who represented the WCO. They began by giving us a brief overview of a WCO project called the Humanity Survival Project. They explained that the purpose is to ensure the survival of the human race by protecting a selected group of people in a hermetically sealed city, possibly for the rest of their lives.

They went on to explain that the purpose of these interviews is to find suitable people who would be willing to join the project. We were being

interviewed because our biometrics identify us to be ideal candidates as scientists in our forties with two children and because of Lucy's notable work.

We were asked numerous questions about our lives, including details about our families, work, and beliefs. We shared information about our upbringing, parents, and how we met and started a family. While they were already aware of our academic accomplishments, they were interested in learning more about our interactions with fellow professors, our hobbies, friendships, and preferences. We provided insights into our social life on and off campus, elaborating on the diverse mix of friends we had and our lack of interest in religion.

After a brief pause for lunch the sociologists offered more details about the project to a group of candidates, "We cannot deny that this endeavour will be incredibly challenging. The city will be subjected to numerous challenges from both within and outside. Initially, living conditions will be austere, with no luxuries, basic food, and a need for everyone to work in unison. Failure to do so would put our survival at risk. Moreover, we must remain vigilant against constant threats from those outside the city who may seek to plunder our resources. As we mentioned before, this undertaking will not be easy."

After bidding us good evening, they handed us a precise outline of the project and asked us to return the next morning to the clinic for medical checks. We had dinner in the hotel and retired to our room. However, we had a fitful night's sleep with many thoughts racing through our minds. The following day, we underwent an extensive medical examination, followed by an interview with four scientists who questioned us about our work and our views on the future.

In the evening, we attended a dinner hosted by the WCO, along with other interviewees. Throughout the dinner, I felt that we were being observed to assess how well we integrated with the group. Following the dinner, we were reminded of the importance of confidentiality and informed that we would receive a response to our interviews within the next two months. If selected, we would be invited to attend a second round of interviews, and we would have two weeks to respond to the invitation.

The two-month wait felt like an eternity. Despite the wait, we were determined to continue with the acceptance process since this was our only hope for a future for our children. However, we regretted that once we entered the city, we would never see our parents again. At this time, they were quite old, and we hoped that nature would take its course

before the chaos of a collapsing world set in, leaving
them to perish with everyone else.

The Interviews

I cannot express how elated we were upon receiving the letter inviting us to the second round of interviews, scheduled to take place at the same venue outside Geneva. The letter outlined that the interview process would span a week and involve rigorous psychological evaluations, which sounded daunting and indeed proved to be so. To our surprise, we were instructed to bring our teenage children along with us. With our bags packed and excited, we embarked on the journey to Geneva. As the train took us through the scenic countryside, reminding us of the beautiful world we will leave behind, we shared stories and jokes to pass the time. We arrived in Geneva filled with hope and anticipation for what lay ahead.

Our first day of the interview process brought unexpected challenges. We were taken to a small studio that seemed barely larger than a closet and told that we would be isolated for three days. The single room was shrouded in darkness, the only light filtering in from a small window near the ceiling. As we searched through the sparse furnishings, we discovered that there was very little food and water available, barely enough to sustain us through our period of isolation. With no way to tell the time or communicate with the outside world, we were left to contemplate our situation in eerie silence. The air was thick with tension, as we struggled to maintain our composure and mental well-being in the face of such isolation. To stave off boredom, we devised various games to play, including spelling contests, quizzes, and guessing games, anything to pass the time and distract us from our predicament.

Our first two nights of isolation proved to be far more challenging than we had anticipated. In the dead of night, we were jolted awake by strange noises and voices that seemed to come from nowhere. The sounds were random and jarring, an assault on our senses that left us feeling disoriented and vulnerable. It was a technique that had been employed in the past as a means of torture, and we could only assume that it was meant to take us to our breaking points. However, because we understood the motive behind it, we were able to resist a complete mental breakdown. Despite our best efforts to remain calm, the experience left us shaken and exhausted. To our surprise, the twins seemed largely unaffected, managing to sleep through most of the commotion. It was a testament to their resilience and fortitude, even in the face of such extreme adversity.

Finally, our three days of isolation came to an end, and we were ushered into a room for interviews with the psychologists. They probed our minds, asking questions that delved into our deepest fears and anxieties. It was an uncomfortable experience, but we understood the importance of the evaluation. The doctors explained that this was just a taste of the difficulties that we might face in our future endeavours. They emphasized that it was essential to have the mental fortitude to overcome challenges, no matter how difficult they might seem. Their words resonated with us, and we left the interview feeling both empowered and humbled. The experience had tested us in ways we could never have imagined, but it had also shown us that we were capable of more than we had ever thought possible.

As the week-long interviews drew to a close, we were presented with a vision of the future that left us breathless with wonder. A team of scientists had been working tirelessly behind the scenes, conducting research and experiments that had culminated in a proposal that was presented to the World Council in 2075. The plan was audacious but also brilliant: to build self-sustaining cities, using the most advanced technologies and renewable energy sources, deep beneath the Earth's surface. These cities would be protected from the harsh conditions on the surface, providing a haven of safety for the select group of people chosen to colonize them. And what a diverse group it would be, representing different races, religions, and cultures, all united in their determination to ensure the survival of the human race. As we listened to the scientists describe their ambitious plan, we felt a sense of hope and optimism that we had never experienced before. It was a vision of the future that we could scarcely imagine, but one that we were honoured to be a part of.

The plan was met with both excitement and apprehension, as it was a huge undertaking that would require massive resources and cooperation from all countries. Despite this, the WCO approved the plan, and the world rallied behind it as it presented a beacon of hope for humanity. In the meantime, efforts to mitigate climate change would continue, with the knowledge that there was a backup plan, thanks to the determination and resilience of the human spirit.

After completing the gruelling psychological evaluations, we were taken to a studio where we experienced a virtual reality simulation of the underground city that would be our new home. The moment the images flickered to life, we were struck by a sense of disorientation and unease. The cavernous space was windowless and artificial, with towering buildings that stretched up to the ceiling, separated by narrow passageways that seemed to twist and turn in impossible ways. The overall effect was disorienting and claustrophobic. There was a distinct lack of green space. As the presentation progressed, we were shown the recreational centres with their state-of-the-art facilities, but even those couldn't shake off the oppressive feeling of being trapped in a pixelated nightmare. We were then shown the industrial and office areas, which were even less inspiring, with rows of cubicles and assembly lines stretching off into infinity. Our initial enthusiasm for the project quickly evaporated, and we discovered later that many others had decided to leave and take their chances in the outside world. Despite our doubts, however, we ultimately decided to stick with the project, knowing that to leave would offer no hope for our children's futures.

Our entire family underwent rigorous mental and medical examinations, including genetic testing, to assess our suitability for the project. It was a nerve-wracking experience, but we held on to the hope that we could be among those selected. As the week progressed, we eagerly awaited the results, then finally, the moment of truth arrived, and we were overjoyed to hear that we had been selected as "saviours of humanity". Tears of relief and gratitude streamed down our faces as we signed the acceptance forms, grateful for the opportunity to play a role in shaping the future of humanity.

We returned home and prepared for the next stage of our journey. We were permitted to take our first step, which was to explain to our parents where we were going and what we would be doing. It was heartbreaking, having to say that we would be saying goodbye, knowing that we would never see them again, and knowing that they would not be able to enjoy their grandchildren. Their reaction was perhaps not so surprising, given the love and devotion they had always shown us, both parents said that they were elated to know that we and the children would survive, and gave us their undying support.

Training

One month after our return home, we received instructions to attend a training facility situated high in the Andes. We learned that the facility had been purpose-built as a training centre and would later serve as accommodation for the construction teams tasked with building self-sustaining cities. The buildings themselves were constructed using 3D printers that utilized sustainable technologies and would eventually be dismantled to make way for defence installations.

During the discussion, a question was raised about whether the buildings in the upcoming cities would resemble the ones we had recently been relocated to. In response, it was clarified that while the new structures would employ the same advanced technology, they would not have the same designs, as they would not need conventional heating or cooling systems. Moreover, they would need to be optimized for the movement of robots, and would offer more spacious living quarters than our current abodes. Additionally, these buildings would be integrated with subterranean transportation systems, and would feature multiple recreational areas for the benefit of the residents.

We were shown to our basic but comfortable quarters located in a block of apartments housing two hundred families. There was everything we needed, with shared facilities for washing, eating, and socialising.

We were informed that we had to live in these basic conditions for six months with the guidance of a team of WCO trainers. One of the first things we learned was how to prepare our food using a Nano-oven, a device to create synthetic food from a variety of protein particles. Although consuming artificially produced food was not new to us, as for several decades the majority of people in developed countries had excluded meat and fish from their diets and were familiar with microbial foods, we couldn't claim to always enjoy eating these products, a sentiment shared by many people, some of whom persisted in eating traditionally produced foods, despite their high cost.

Water was rationed to the point where there was barely enough for washing ourselves or our clothes. The clothing we were issued was made of non-invasive micro-fibres that required very little water to clean and did not need any detergents. We were not provided with soap or other cleansing products to wash our bodies, and we were instructed to use water only on visibly dirty areas. This practice was meant to encourage friendly microbes to live in symbiotic harmony on our skin by feasting on the ammonia from our sweat and creating low-maintenance, balanced skin. While there were many unpleasant odours at first, they dissipated within a month, although we may have simply got used to them. We were reminded that this was the new way of life in our world and that we needed to adapt.

As the facilities served the entire block, we were instructed to form work groups to carry out various tasks. Over four weeks, we received training on food preparation, distribution logistics, maintenance, security procedures, and the principles of governance in our future world. It was emphasized that this knowledge would be essential for our survival.

The social model we were going to live under would not be driven by a monetary system. Instead, work would be performed to benefit the community without financial rewards. There would be no currency or purchasing system. At first, it was hard to imagine a world without money, but as they explained, if we were to live in a micro-world driven by competitive forces, it would lead to a condensed version of the world we live in today. Besides, there will be nothing available to purchase, everyone will receive the materials required for their comfort and survival. Our world will be completely different

from the world we will leave behind. Our minds will be focused on doing everything necessary to stay alive, and the idea of competitiveness will not have a place in our lives as we work hard together and be motivated by the common goal of survival. We will develop new incentives to suit the new environment.

To avoid developing an association with a location, and to prevent territorial allegiances or rivalries, the residents of the apartment block were encouraged to mix with families from different blocks. As part of the social engineering plan, we, like others, were moved to different blocks during our stay.

Those six months demonstrated what our existence would be like for the remainder of our lives. For some, the idea of living in an enclosed environment was too much, and they decided to leave the project. The children quickly formed friendships and submerged themselves in their schooling, which as they represented the next generation of survivors, were focused on the skills that they would need when it was their turn.

It was explained that the robots accompanying us throughout our tenancy were 3rd generation robots, numbering approximately one to every five people. Their role is to undertake manual tasks and assist with teaching our children. Updated versions will accompany us into the city to help us through the difficult times that lay ahead.

Final Preparations

After six months, we received a briefing that provided more details about our future lives. During the briefing, we were shown a model of a Martian city that had been designed in the 2040s as a way for humanity to escape extinction. Although it was never built, the city's design included several innovative technologies for producing materials and nutrients from available elements which were originally developed to support a small settlement that existed on the Moon for a few years.

The WCO representatives explained that they were near completing six cities with a further four to follow. Each city will be built to house approximately 60,000 people, with the possibility to increase that to 200,000 in the future if it is thought necessary. Security surrounding the building of the cities will be tight, and few people will know of the project and the locations of the cities. We ask you to keep your involvement secret to avoid being put under pressure from people, politicians, oligarchs, and even criminals, who will want to live in the cities. We are only interviewing people with appropriate skills, who could survive the harsh conditions and bring value to the communities.

The cities will be built into the sides of remote mountainous areas and equipped with sophisticated defence systems. Each city will be capable of producing its air and energy through the use of nuclear fusion reactors and geothermal sources.

There were concerns raised about the prospect of living in vast cave-like dwellings for decades or possibly even centuries. However, the project representatives assured us that suitable locations outside of the cities would be constructed as soon as it was safe to do so. Unfortunately, they were unable to provide a specific time frame due to the numerous uncertainties surrounding the project.

It was unsurprising to learn that some experts predict the collapse of mankind could be preceded by the collapse of large parts of the world's biosphere. But then an anthropologist went on to hypothesize that a partial collapse of the biosphere together with the other stresses caused by climate change could exacerbate existing social and economic tensions, leading to conflict and ultimately humanity's self-destruction. If this were to happen, then the resulting reduction in population and the accompanying decrease in anthropogenic activities would reduce the possibility of a total collapse of the Earth's biosphere. This could allow the survival of many of the Earth's ecological systems, in contrast to the fate of humanity. This is a good reason to increase our efforts to protect our environment as much as possible and as quickly as possible.

During the discussion, a question was raised about how the supply of fresh water would be ensured. In response, it was explained that freshwater would be obtained from adjacent lakes or underground reservoirs, harvested rainwater, and desalinated saltwater where possible. Water usage management would be implemented to reduce water consumption, and recycling would play a critical role in ensuring sustainable use.

During the group discussion, I asked how the atmosphere would be maintained. The response was interesting. "Filtered air from the outside will be enriched with oxygen produced as a by-product of hydrogen gas production. The hydrogen gas will be used to heat the atmosphere and keep a consistent temperature throughout the city. This approach will eliminate the need for domestic heating and weather-dependent clothing."

From the back of the room came a question: "How will we be able to sustain the production of the equipment that will be needed to run our cities?' The response was intriguing. "There will be a moratorium on developing new technologies for the foreseeable future. However, each city will have modern state-of-the-art production facilities, manned by robots and equipped with vast resources of natural materials. These will address the basic needs for our survival for several decades by which time it is anticipated that we will be able to obtain materials from the outside world. Keep in mind that many of the luxuries we take for granted today, such as mobile phones, cars, and televisions, will no longer be available in the cities. We must prepare ourselves for a simpler life, akin to that of the Victorians, but with the modern technologies that will support our existence". At first, I was shocked by this revelation, but the more I thought about it, the more I began to appreciate the idea of living in a simpler, more sustainable society.

During the speech, the speaker highlighted the commitment to achieving a zero-waste goal for the cities. They stated that all waste generated by the city would be recycled, reused, or repurposed sustainably. They plan to use sewage as a source of nutrients for the city's gardens and items that are no longer needed will be passed on to others, recycled, or repurposed to create new items, aligning with their target of a circular economy. This initiative is one of their top priorities.

The next question came from a young boy. "Will we be able to play with our friends?" "Yes, definitely, there will be playgrounds with skateparks, bicycling trails, swings and roundabouts, and much more to come."

Barely had she finished when another child stood up. "Will there be ice cream and chocolate?" "I'm afraid not at first, but there will be toys and as soon as we can, you will have ice cream, chocolates, cakes and a lot more."

We were informed that the documentation provided would answer most, if not all, of our questions. As we read through it, the reality of our future became increasingly clear. Initially, we felt apprehensive about the significant changes to our lives that we would have to undergo, but as we reflected on the extensive training we had received, we gained confidence in our ability to adapt and survive. Though the idea of living underground for an extended period was daunting and unsettling, the prospect of a slow and painful demise in the outside world made it easier to accept.

The representatives from the WCO provided information on how we can prepare for the next phase of our journey by spending up to a year in a holding complex. "During this time, you will be living in conditions similar to what you can expect when you arrive at your final destination. However, it's important to note that this is not a training exercise, and you will not have the support of training personnel during your stay. It's crucial that you take this time seriously and use it to become fully prepared for your new lives, as there will be no turning back once you reach your final destination. It's important to keep your eyes on the ultimate goal".

On the day of our transfer, we were taken to a three-bedroom apartment close to the training facility. We had been preparing for this moment for six months, but the reality of leaving behind friends and familiar surroundings was still difficult, especially for the twins. We were instructed to bring only a few personal belongings, as we would be issued with clothing that was recyclable, stain-resistant, and suitable for a constant climate. This was necessary to reduce our environmental impact and ensure our comfort during our underground stay.

Without our previous training in adapting to the limitations of our new life, the thought of never again being able to shower daily and the limited, flavourless food options would have been daunting.

The information document explained how everyone will be assigned to a city and their living quarters as soon as they are ready. In the coming days, we will all receive a rota detailing the daily tasks that we need to familiarize ourselves with.

The system of governance was inspiring. The goal of the new world was to eliminate politics, exclude a monetary economy, and create a fair and equitable society. This Utopian world was something I had only ever dreamt of.

Everything we read reinforced our determination to continue with our new life. It gave us a sense of pioneering spirit as if we were destined to create a new world order and save mankind from extinction.

Entering Cima

Our city, called Cima, is buried deep into the side of a mountain, located in a remote area of the Pyrenees Atlantic known as Cima Ezkurra.

I have never forgotten that day in 2083, July 15th to be precise, when we entered the huge glass dome at the entrance of Cima and were transported through a tunnel into what was to be our world. We were both overwhelmed with a feeling of veneration and wonderment at what had been achieved. The behemoth size of the city, the designs of the building and corridors, the hustle and bustle of people, the noises, the smells, and everything about our new world left us in awe. The sheer magnitude of the logistics of selecting and training 600,000 people, and moving them into ten cities within 10 years, must have been phenomenal.

It was reassuring to see the people who had guided us throughout our journey, were there to greet us, knowing they would oversee the governance of Cima until the system is established.

Our apartment, located in the heart of Cima, was surprisingly spacious, featuring three cosy bedrooms, a bathroom, and two toilets. The compact yet functional kitchen was equipped with all the necessities, allowing us to prepare simple but nutritious meals. The living room was modestly furnished with a comfortable couch and a small coffee table, but it provided a welcoming space for us to relax and unwind. One of the highlights of our apartment was the small terrace that overlooked the vibrant artificial gardens surrounding the apartment blocks. Despite being a man-made creation, the gardens were teeming with colourful flowers, lush greenery, and even a few chirping birds, providing a much-needed respite from the sterile environment of the underground city.

The first few days were spent familiarising ourselves with our surroundings, and getting to know our domestic robot who was introduced to us as Zal609, and responded to the name Zal. It was Zal's first job to get to know us. During our interviews, Zal questioned us about food preferences, our times for going to bed and the times we usually rose, questions about our characters, and what were our likes and dislikes. Zal, 'He', as we decided to gender it, spent the time he wasn't occupied, standing by the recharging station in the hallway.

At first, Zal prepared our food in a Nanofabricator cooker, the updated version of the Nanoven, selecting from a limited choice of dishes. Later we decided that we would take over preparing our evening meals, just so that we could make our own choices, including the accompanying beverages. Zal collected the ingredients for producing our meals from the laboratories where the protein molecules were produced. He cleaned the dishes in the steamer and kept the apartment clean. Cleanliness was essential to prevent the spread of sickness and disease, which could easily overwhelm the limited medical facilities.

Our first excursion was to attend a symposium that was held in a community centre located three blocks from our dwelling. Zal accompanied us through the passageways that connected the buildings and showed us how to request a travel pod, as well as how to command it to take us to our destination. After ensuring that we understood the process, he returned to the apartment, leaving us to continue the journey on our own.

On our arrival, the organisers warmly welcomed us and invited us to help ourselves to refreshments. The selection of drinks and small treats on offer was a pleasant surprise, as we had not yet explored the full extent of what the Nanoven could provide. The meeting room was spacious and bustling, with what seemed like at least a thousand attendees mingling, sipping, and chatting.

Shortly after everyone had settled in, a woman who we recognised as one of our tutors, stood on the podium and delivered a speech on how we are to survive in our new world without upsetting each other.

"During the first few years, we will all be busy with our allotted tasks and focused on survival. It is important to understand that we need each other to survive, we can not afford to think only of ourselves or our families, we have to think of ourselves as part of the community, because unless we do, I assure you, none of us will survive".

She went on to explain how we could achieve this through social integration, by avoiding nationalistic and religious prejudices, and by seeing everyone as equal.

"I cannot emphasize enough the importance of what we are doing. Apart from violence and the collapse of our society through social unrest, there are several other reasons why our survival may fail. Our healthcare capabilities will be very limited during the first few years, so staying healthy is of paramount importance. We must control our weight and maintain our fitness. Any signs of sickness must be immediately reported, as communicable diseases can spread rapidly through our enclosed environment and affect everyone. The threat of external forces overcoming our city is real, so we must ensure our defensive systems remain diligent and alert at all times. Lastly, there is always a possibility of our city being destroyed by natural disasters such as earthquakes and volcanic eruptions. This is why there are ten cities, and the hope is that at least one will survive."

Then another speaker continued. "I would like to introduce myself, my name is Pooja. I'll be responsible for cross-cultural communications during the first few years. If you have questions or concerns that you wish to discuss, please do not hesitate to contact me. All of our contact details are found in the information packs. I would like to point out that the language Franca spoken in all of the ten cities, will be the modernized international version of English. We can, and probably will, continue using our native language in our private lives, but communications outside of that environment will be in English."

As the speakers finished, the silence was deafening, everyone in that room wanted to be the ones who would survive.

Familiarisation

Those first months were hard. Much of our time was taken up with fulfilling our duties which for Lucy and me were largely overseeing the newly installed supply networks and developing rotas. Everything was new to us, often leading to heightened tensions as things, as they frequently did, go wrong. This led to occasional disputes between colleagues and family members. Most times they were about trivial differences and were quickly resolved amongst the parties involved, but there were occasions when a mediator was brought in to settle the dispute. Reminding people about the consequences of social discourse helped to ease tensions and made disputes rare.

Coordinating the activities of 60,000 people was a monumental challenge, compounded by frequent technical failures and human errors that disrupted services and created additional tension. Once educational facilities were established, people were able to break out of their daily routines and engage in a different environment for part of the day. This provided a much-needed boost by offering a diverse range of learning opportunities and activities and helped alleviate some of the stresses of daily life.

The diverse range of tasks we were assigned during the initial period aimed to acquaint us with the workings of the city and give us an appreciation of the complexities involved in our city lives. While the robots were responsible for most tasks, from operating and maintaining highly automated production facilities to running medical and welfare services, it was our responsibility to learn about the processes by overseeing them and understanding what was going on in and around our city. The thought and planning that had gone into the infrastructure were extraordinary, resulting in a perfectly balanced, albeit unnatural, environment that functioned seamlessly.

In the centre of the city, there were numerous fitness and recreational facilities, including swimming pools and exercise rooms. As time passed, additional amenities were added, such as social clubs, restaurants, squash, and tennis courts. Despite the availability of these facilities, after a year of living in Cima, many of us began to suffer from claustrophobia. The lack of exposure to natural light and the outside world was taking its toll. We were not alone in our feelings; many people were experiencing some form of depression. To prevent the spread of discontent, therapy and medication were offered to everyone. Additionally, we were reassured that things would improve in the coming year.

Our New World

After conducting a series of social experiments focused on collectivism, we successfully created a stable and functional environment. By emphasizing the importance of working together and valuing the needs of the community over individual desires, we were able to foster a sense of unity and cooperation among our group. However, we were reminded of the challenges that still lay ahead during a symposium where a speaker discussed the need for continued effort to maintain our progress. Despite the obstacles we faced, we remained committed to our collective goals and worked tirelessly to overcome any obstacles that arose.

She continued to say "over the next few decades, we anticipate significant changes in the lives of people living outside of our cities. If current trends continue, there is a risk of increased conflict and violence, both within and between countries, as competition for resources like food and water intensifies. In such a scenario, societal and economic collapse could lead to an increase in lawlessness and insecurity, which could destabilize governments and threaten the fabric of civilization. While the outcome is uncertain, we believe that proactive steps can be taken to mitigate the risks and help ensure our future. To avoid the possibility of ongoing territorial disputes, Paeancea, the name given to our new world, has been designed without countries or a capital city. Instead, it functions as a global diaspora of peacefully united families who share equal beliefs and standards".

She then went on to explain "the name Paeancea is a portmanteau derived from the words Pangaea, a single ancient continent, Paean, meaning a song of thanksgiving, and Panacea, meaning a remedy for all ills. Together, the name represents the central ideology of our new world, which emphasizes unity, equality, and peace. Cima is just one of ten cities that comprise Paeancea".

After hearing about the vision for Paeancea, the room was filled with a sense of excitement and anticipation. We all felt like pioneers embarking on a journey to build a better world, a utopia that would be like a modern-day Garden of Eden. The energy in the room was palpable, as everyone was filled with pride, joy, and passionate enthusiasm to fulfil their destinies as part of this new community. As we shared our ideas and hopes for the future, it became clear that we were part of something truly special, and that together we could create a world that was truly worth living in.

The speaker continued, "the ten cities that comprise the United Nation of Paeancea are roughly the same size and population. Each location for the cities have been carefully selected for its sustainable supply of freshwater and self-sufficiency in all aspects. These cities communicated with each other through satellite links, creating a network that spanned the entire globe. The locations have been strategically chosen to provide the cities with optimal defensive capabilities, ensuring the safety and security of all citizens in the face of potential threats". As we learned more about these other cities, it became clear that Paeancea was not just a single entity, but a complex and interconnected system that had been designed to thrive in a world where cooperation and resilience were paramount.

The speaker went on to describe the ten cities of Paeancea, "each named after the region where it is located. Calama, buried deep in the Andes Mountains, was once the site of a mining company. Potala, located in the Himalayas near Tibet, took its name from the ancient palace of the Dalai Lamas. Rinjani, on a small Indonesian island named after the extinct volcano that looms over it. Altai, located in Central Asia, is situated near the point where Russia, China, Mongolia, and Kazakhstan converged. Komi, buried deep in the Urals, is named after the surrounding area. Vulcan, nestled in the Carpathian Mountains of Eastern Europe, is named after the Roman god of fire. Mauna Kea, located on one of the Hawaiian Islands, takes its name from the mountain on which it is built. Borough, situated in the Australian Alps, is named after the boroughs of London. Franz, the ninth city, is located in Greenland. And finally, our city, Cima, is situated in the heart of the Pyrenees."

A question that had been on everyone's mind was finally asked by someone in the audience. "Can you give us an idea of when it will be safe to leave the cities?" An American sociologist stood up to respond. "As you can imagine, there are many uncertainties and our predictions have a wide margin of error. Based on our modelling, we anticipate that by 2100, the Earth's temperature will have risen by approximately 4.0 degrees Celsius above pre-industrial levels. This will trigger wars between neighbouring countries, particularly those with large populations, as they compete for access to water and arable land. The movement of people from impoverished regions and flooded coastal regions will also become increasingly violent and devastating. We estimate that this process will unfold over around 50 years, during which the world's population will plummet to less than two million. Once the worst of the violence has subsided, and with adequate protection, it may be possible to venture outside the safety of our enclosures."

A second question came from another member of the audience, "What will happen to people living outside of our cities who manage to survive the holocaust?"

The same speaker continued, "We cannot make any guarantees for those who do not share our values of peace, equality, and unity. We have spent many years building this world and we will not allow it to be threatened by those who seek to disrupt it. Therefore, those who wish to join us will have to undergo a screening process to ensure that they do not pose a threat to our community. This process will be fair and just, and we will only accept those who share our values and can contribute positively to our society".

Our Routine Lives

The years crept by slowly, especially in the beginning when each day felt indistinguishable from the last. Cut off from the outside world, we were confined to an existence where day and night blended, and weekends lost their meaning. It became increasingly difficult to keep track of the days of the week or even the changing seasons.

We were each assigned a rotating schedule to ensure that some individuals were always working while others could enjoy the city's social amenities. Despite the considerable effort put into designing this system, boredom remained a constant threat. In the first few years, there were ten reported suicides and numerous conflicts that were attributed to cabin fever. Those affected received psychological counselling and medication as needed, but to my knowledge, no one chose to leave the city.

Apart from our work as virologists, during those first years, we had other responsibilities that were not entirely related to our education. About half of the time, we carried out mundane tasks that were rarely interesting. Despite this, we undertook them happily, knowing how important they were to the survival of Cima.

During our second year in Cima, we had the opportunity to experience the artificial environment of the newly created Greenhouse, which was a large glass dome adjacent to the city. It was populated with a variety of plants, beautiful birds, and even some small mammals. The Greenhouse was designed to provide some relief from our troglodyte existence. Our first visit to the Greenhouse was the first time in two years that we had experienced natural light and could witness the weather and seasons. Since we followed the lunar calendar based on the local time zone in our artificial world, we didn't need to adjust.

The Greenhouse is a controlled environment that is protected from pathogens and external threats, with an artificially created atmosphere to maintain the necessary conditions for life. Visitors are instructed on evacuation procedures as a precautionary measure against potential attacks. It serves as a vital source of relief for the visitors, who eagerly anticipate the three invitations they receive each year offering them a lifeline for their mental health and well-being, helping to relieve the monotony of their everyday lives

I think it was in the third year when we began to grow accustomed to our way of life and even, for the most part, enjoy it. Our lives started to take on new objectives. Instead of solely focusing our energies on work, we pursued hobbies, made new friendships, and engaged in further educational studies. We were now emerging from the fog of our everyday lives, witnessing the creation of an ethos of altruistic community living that resembled the Confucian ideal of Ren. Ren is a behaviour that a person exhibits to promote a flourishing human community.

The government expanded educational and medical facilities to meet the needs of our growing population and asked families to limit their size to a maximum of three children, which was largely observed. For us, the request was irrelevant, as we had made the decision decades ago to have only two children. Now, in our fifties, we had no regrets about our choice.

The Apocalypse

As the century drew to a close, the world entered a new phase of threats to its very existence. Many of the problems predicted at least seventy years earlier had now come to pass. From our vantage point, we watched in horror as civilizations and economies collapsed across the globe. Tragic events unfolded before our eyes, signalling a dark and uncertain future for humanity.

Lucy and I were part of a team tasked with monitoring the apocalyptic events unfolding in Western Europe. We were appalled by the swift collapse of entire civilizations and their political, social, and economic structures, which were swiftly replaced by a dystopian landscape of hostility and despair. It was jarring to see how quickly the veneer of culture and civilization crumbled, as people regressed to their primal instincts.

The dystopian societies that emerged in the wake of civilization's collapse wreaked havoc on the supply chains of essential services and products. As violence and lawlessness became the norm, humanity descended into a downward spiral from which there seemed to be no escape. Millions of migrants, with nothing left to lose, risked everything to fight their way into neighbouring countries, adding to the already overcrowded conditions caused by domestic migrants fleeing flooded coastal towns.

Famine and disease were rampant across the globe, compounding the already dire situation. The rise of terrorism and mass migrations into diasporic communities only fueled violent conflicts between unwelcome migrants and weakening authorities. As the breakdown of law and order continued, even the largest cities were unable to withstand the chaos.

Newly-formed terrorist groups carried out arbitrary acts of bioterrorism, introducing deadly pathogenic agents that compounded the already dire situation. In addition, zoonotic bacteria and viruses, which had returned with the chaotic migrations, spread unchecked among the overcrowded communities, resulting in sickness and death on an unprecedented scale. The development and distribution of vaccines proved impossible in the face of such a rapidly spreading contagion.

At this point, the world's economies had all but crumbled, and as many as four billion people had perished in the chaos. The few countries that had managed to maintain some level of stability were being toppled by one putsch after another, leading to anarchy and conflict with neighbouring nations as they scrambled to seize whatever resources remained.

The alliances that once held the world together were now crumbling as governments collapsed under the weight of unprecedented pressures. Armed conflicts to secure life-saving resources broke out between nations, leading to a third-world war. The initial spark occurred when Pakistan and India engaged in a nuclear conflict over dwindling freshwater supplies, as the rivers that ran through their lands began to dry up following the meltdown of Himalayan glaciers that fed them. Israel and Iran soon joined the fray, followed by other nuclear powers, until the entire world was engulfed in conflict, leaving billions dead and displaced in its wake.

Witnessing the scale and ferocity of the disintegration of mankind was heartbreaking, causing many to feel guilt for surviving. One family traumatized by the events committed suicide, and I suffered bouts of deep depression, as the pictures of the horrors played back through my mind. I was awakened at night by vivid nightmares visualising the detritus of civilizations, of bodies rotting in the streets, of living corpses fighting over scraps of food, and of the chaos and mayhem that played out in cities. Despite counselling, I have continued to relive these scenes throughout my life.

The collapse of Earth's biodiversity has been occurring for more than two centuries, and unfortunately, the disintegration of society happened in a mere fifty years. Despite the world's vast scientific, technological, and creative resources, they failed to prevent the world from crumbling into disarray.

Our efforts to insure the survival of humanity became even more resolute.

My Retirement

As a 95-year-old widower, I look back on my life with gratitude and a deep sense of love for my lifelong partner, Lucy. She passed away five years ago due to age-related causes. Despite the challenges we faced during our years of confinement, our years together were amazing, and we remained committed to our work for the betterment of humanity and our children's future. Throughout our lives, our children have been a constant source of support for our well-being, and they continue to believe in the importance of Paeancean ideals.

In the early spring of 2078, the twins Cleo and Henry met their partners, and after a few months moved into their apartments. In 2080, Cleo and her partner Jack presented Lucy and me with a grandchild, a healthy boy named after my father, Alvin, and five years later they had Genny, a beautiful girl. Our third grandchild, Laetitia, came along in 2083, a beautiful child born to Henry and his partner Samantha.

Lucy and I retired shortly after the birth of Alvin and were immediately enrolled in the age-old tradition of the grandparents babysitting, which we fitted in with our retirement project, which was volunteering to assist undergraduates with their research work.

As first-generation Paeanceans, we had limited education choices, but we passed on the knowledge we had acquired to the next generation. Our ultimate goal was to improve living conditions, which included enhancing medical and defensive systems and increasing food and energy production. The second generation's responsibility was to develop new technologies to improve their lives and establish their place in this new world.

Chapter Two

Second Generation

As I write this, it is the year 2140, and I am an octogenarian named Henry. My wife Samantha and I have spent most of our lives living inside a cave, shielded from the harsh realities of the outside world. My twin sister Cleo and I joined our parents in Cima when we were twenty, back in 2083. Now, eighteen years since my father finished his memoirs, I feel it is time for me to share my own experiences of life in this new world. So, let me take you on a journey of discovery through the development of Cima and the challenges we have faced as a society.

My memories of life outside Cima are hazy, much like my father's. However, I have maintained a meticulous diary since my early days here, documenting every vital event and emotion. These journals will serve as vivid reminders of the 57 intervening years, allowing me to share my story with you in greater detail. From the struggles of adapting to a new way of life to moments of joy and triumph, my diary captures it all. I am excited to share my experiences with you and shed light on what it's like to grow up and live in a world like Cima.

The first-generation families, including my parents, have given us a world that is peaceful, fulfilling, and comfortable. They had to make a difficult transition from a lifestyle that allowed many freedoms to an underground existence with many restrictions. They accepted this change because they recognized the importance of saving the human race from extinction. This transition was challenging for most people, but their sacrifices allowed us to enjoy a world where friendships thrive, and we can live our lives in relative comfort and a stable foundation upon which to build.

Throughout my father's lifetime, we have witnessed remarkable progress in improving our living standards. One such example is the expansion of Cima, which has allowed for a more spacious and comfortable living environment. Additionally, we now have access to a secured outdoor recreational area, which has added an immeasurable quality to our lives. While leaving the city limits is restricted to those who need to travel for work, transfer to other Paeancean cities, or join organized ecotourism trips, we are grateful for the opportunity to venture beyond our city. Flights are carried out under strict security measures to protect against potential attacks, but the benefits of experiencing the beauty of our world are worth the extra precautions.

Our living quarters have undergone significant upgrades, providing us with more space and better equipment. One of the most exciting additions is the 3rd generation Nano-oven, which offers an incredible range of flavours, textures, and visualizations, inspiring us to experiment with new recipes and share them with friends. In addition, it's exciting to see that restaurants serving reproductions of classic dishes from the past are now popping up in community centres and outdoor recreational areas. These restaurants, like most things in Cima, are managed by robots under human supervision, ensuring consistent and efficient service delivery. It's remarkable to think how far we've come since the early days of our underground existence, and I can't wait to see what the future holds for us in terms of culinary advancements.

As second-generation Paeanceans, we don't have a clear idea of what normality means because our lives have been shaped by a different set of circumstances. Instead, we focus on making progress and improving our quality of life, one step at a time. While my father has shared that we can never go back to the way things were before if we want to continue surviving, we don't see this as a negative thing. Instead, we embrace the opportunities that come with change and strive to create a better future for ourselves and future generations.

Life Outside Of Cima

As I have mentioned before, life outside of the cities is treacherous. There are still many thousands of people scattered around the world who are struggling to survive. They have limited access to medical facilities and are constantly searching for food and water to sustain themselves. The ravages of disease, coupled with a low birth rate and high child mortality, make their future uncertain. Despite their plight, they remain a potential threat to those who live in the cities.

In just fifty years over eight billion people died, leaving the global population at less than 1.5 million by 2150. Pandemics ravaged the planet, with the spread of infectious diseases being the primary cause of death. Unfortunately, some of these diseases are still pandemic today and may continue to affect us indefinitely.

It's remarkable how quickly the Earth's ecosystem has recovered since the extinction event. The world's non-Paeancean cities have disappeared due to rising sea levels, encroaching deserts, or decaying into ruins that have been reclaimed by nature. However, the farmlands that managed to survive the floods have undergone a natural rewilding process, with both flora and fauna returning.

Numerous species of insects and birds, which were on the verge of extinction, have reappeared, along with many smaller mammals. Unfortunately, most larger mammal species became extinct, but there's hope that they can be reintroduced someday, thanks to DNA collected by our forebears. Marine life has also made a remarkable recovery, now that human activities are no longer decimating their populations.

The landscape has undergone dramatic changes, with many of the world's great rivers and lakes disappearing due to persistent droughts or the melting of glaciers that once fed them. In their place, vast expanses of arid, windswept terrain have emerged. However, there have also been some unexpected transformations, with new lakes and rivers forming in regions that have been subjected to frequent flooding. Rising sea levels have had a profound impact on coastlines, causing the disappearance of thousands of islands and reshaping entire continents. Both poles have lost more than 70% of their ice cover, but areas that were once frozen wasteland are now lush green wildernesses. Despite these changes, it is likely to take thousands of years for the planet to fully recover from the effects of climate change.

Through our advanced surveillance systems, we have observed that there are only a few remaining areas on the planet where farming is still practised. The once orderly and meticulously maintained hedgerows that delineated the fields have now given way to a wild tangle of trees and bushes. Amidst the overgrowth, we can still see remnants of human-built structures, although it is evident that they will eventually succumb to the relentless march of nature. To preserve our past and ensure that future generations can appreciate our history, archaeologists have already begun the vital task of safeguarding significant cultural sites.

Despite the widespread devastation caused by the holocaust, small pockets of aboriginal communities have managed to survive relatively unscathed. These communities have been discovered living on remote islands and in secluded forests, and it appears that their isolation and traditional knowledge have allowed them to adapt to the changes and avoid the worst impacts of the pandemics and violence. Their resilience and resourcefulness provide hope for their future, and efforts are being made to respect and preserve their cultures and knowledge.

Toxic chemicals and microplastic particles remain major environmental hazards, contaminating our rivers, oceans, and the air we breathe. Despite the lack of effective solutions, we can observe how life is adapting to these dangerous threats. Some species are evolving to tolerate or even thrive in polluted environments, while others are changing their behaviour or migrating to safer habitats. However, we must continue to develop and implement sustainable practices to reduce the impact of human activities on the environment and ensure a healthier future for all living beings.

Despite the decline in human-caused carbon emissions and the emergence of natural carbon sinks, the melting arctic tundra and oceans continue to release significant amounts of CO_2 and methane into the atmosphere. As a result, the climate is still slowly warming and continues to plague the planet with violent storms, droughts, flooding, and extreme temperatures. It is forecasted to persist for hundreds of years until the Earth's temperature returns to its early twenty-first-century levels. Although efforts are being made to address these environmental challenges, the scope and scale of the problem mean it will take several generations to repair the damage.

Lost Paeancean Cities

In 2093, the city of Komi located in the Urals was attacked by military forces, in violation of international agreements. Despite the city's defences holding back the attacks for several weeks, the well-armed and determined force eventually broke through. The few survivors recounted the horrific events that followed, soldiers killing anyone they encountered and looting everything they could carry, with no intention of occupying the city. Unfortunately, at that time we were unable to assist, leaving the survivors to their fate alongside those living outside of our cities.

A second catastrophic event struck a decade later when an earthquake decimated the city of Mauna Kea in Hawaii. The mountain containing the city imploded in an instant, leaving few survivors. While our city has been targeted by small armed groups on multiple occasions, consisting mostly of poorly armed aggressors numbering between 10 and >1,000, our defence networks have been able to detect and neutralize them swiftly, leaving very few to recount their tale. However, with improved mobility and upgraded defence systems, we can now offer aid to other cities in need.

Earth's Population

The question of whether to allow unrestrained population growth now that the planet has recovered to a degree or to continue setting a cap has been a recurring issue that we as Paeanceans must address in every generation. To gain a deeper understanding of its implications, we have turned to the original concept of Paeancea created by some of the world's greatest minds. We have incorporated parts of this document into our Constitution as a blueprint for our future, not as a mandate, but as a guide. The extensive list of pros and cons for each recommended action provides our planners with valuable insights for their decision-making processes, given that the creators of Paeancea had a better understanding of the challenges in their world.

The paper analyzed every aspect of population density and its impact on both human evolution and the well-being of the planet. Its conclusion was clear: we should not allow unrestrained population growth. We have learned from the mistakes of the past and cannot trust humanity to dominate the planet's ecology again. Therefore, we must continue to regulate the Earth's population level to ensure that it remains sustainable for generations to come.

Paeancea has a population of approximately 980,000, with each city having around 110,000 residents. It is possible to increase the population of each city by 90,000 within a generation, given our current estimated reproduction rate of 1.25 and average lifespan of 90 years. However, this would require a significant investment of manpower and resources, as well as potentially adding pressure to the harmonious relationships between the cities due to increased population density. Therefore, to achieve further population growth, it would be necessary to either increase the capacity of existing cities or build new ones, which are currently beyond our capabilities.

Paeancea's existing gene pool is diverse enough to sustain us in the foreseeable future, and our population level is sufficient to enable us to carry out all necessary tasks and continue researching for our future. The decision to maintain our population level between 900,000 and 1,100,000 was reached through a referendum. With this population range, we have the necessary capacity to manage all aspects of running our community and maintain a healthy and sustainable environment for generations to come.

Population control is a topic of heated debate in our community every five years, with pragmatists and liberalists taking opposing stances. The pragmatists advocate for immediate, coercive measures to be taken against families who exceed the recommended number of offspring, while the liberalists prefer to utilize soft power through education and persuasion. The liberalists prevailed, but it is acknowledged that repeat offenders who breach the recommended birth rate target may face small penalties. This compromise allows for a balanced approach to population control that considers both individual rights and the sustainability of our community.

Our family has only had one offspring, keeping our family size within acceptable limits. Despite this, as we age, we continue to enjoy good health and remain productive members of society. Our reproductive age limit has remained unchanged, leading to an increasing ratio of older people to those of childbearing age. This demographic shift will likely result in a significant drop in birth rates in the near future. Therefore, at present, our emphasis is on encouraging people to have more children by increasing the recommended birth rate. This strategy aims to address the impending decline in population and maintain a balanced demographic structure within our community.

It has been mutually agreed upon that the target boundaries shall undergo a review process in five

years, during which modifications may be made if
deemed necessary.

Egalitarianism

Our Constitution reflects our commitment to secular and nonpartisan values. At the core of our political and social doctrine lies Egalitarianism, the belief that every person is equal and should be treated as such. Although this idea has been pursued for centuries, it has never been fully realized until now. Through the removal of economic inequalities and decentralization of governmental power, we have achieved equal access to political, economic, social, and civil rights.

It is worth mentioning the role of religion in our contemporary society. In our secular society, Egalitarianism serves as our guiding principle and social philosophy, though it is not a religion in the traditional sense as it does not involve worship or deities, it has replaced the religious doctrines of our ancestors. Some individuals may still hold onto private beliefs that are not expressed publicly.

As Paeanceans, our austere beginnings have given rise to a shared social philosophy that unites us. We are a cohesive society that has evolved with the belief that we not only save ourselves but also contribute to the greater good of humankind. To this day, we uphold a frugal lifestyle, avoiding waste and eschewing the pursuit of personal possessions.

My father likened Egalitarianism to a humane version of communism without the advocacies of free-market systems and self-appointed machiavellian leaders to bring about their downfall.

Paeancean Governance

The foundation of our governance systems can be traced back to the "Fundamental Principles of Governance" outlined in the Treaty of Paeancea, established by the founders of our nation. While these systems have evolved and will continue to do so in the future, they remain rooted in the three key provisions that reflect the essence of Paeancea as a unified country with eight equally significant cities, where everyone is treated equally and no competition exists between economies. This is reinforced by the absence of a monetary system, which underscores our commitment to fairness and cooperation.

The Fundamental Principles of Governance, as established in the Treaty of Paeancea, consist of three core provisions that form the bedrock of our nation's political system. Firstly, the provision that there shall be a single Parliament that unites all of our cities, without creating any divisive barriers. Secondly, we do not have political leaders or elected representatives in power, as we believe in a system where everyone has an equal voice. Thirdly, our constitution serves as the cornerstone of all decision-making processes, ensuring that our government is always grounded in legal principles and fairness.

The founding Constitution of our nation embodies three fundamental principles of governance: Egalitarianism, Meritocracy, and Stability. In addition to these core principles, it also encompasses a comprehensive framework for environmental governance, including Population Control, protection, and regeneration of the Earth's ecosystems, as well as Technological Evolution. The Constitution also addresses the Juridical system, providing governance for security issues, asset protection, behavioural norms, crime prevention, and correctional measures. By including these critical elements, our Constitution provides a comprehensive blueprint for the responsible governance of our society and the environment.

While the Constitution does not explicitly address issues related to social cohesion, well-being, and lifestyle, any actions taken to address these concerns must comply with the principles outlined in the Constitution. The governance of the Constitution is also outlined within the document and has been invoked on numerous occasions. Our current governance structure is reminiscent of that of our ancestors, with a Parliamentary committee at the helm, followed by the Legislature, Juridical, and Executive Committees. The Executive Committee oversees eight Representational Committees that serve as representatives of the eight cities.

For any new legislation to be put into effect, it must first receive majority approval from all twelve committees. If it fails to gain the necessary support, it will be either rejected outright or sent back for further amendments. While this process may seem cumbersome, it plays a crucial role in safeguarding against the undue influence of any individual or group over our lives.

In fulfilling our civic duties, both Samantha and I have proudly served on Cima's Representational and Parliamentary Committees. Additionally, Samantha has lent her expertise to the Juridical Committee, while I have served on the Executive Committee. Together, we have amassed a collective service record of 17 years, surpassing the recommended commitment of 5 to 15 years that every citizen is expected to fulfil in service of Paeancea's governance.

Both of us are committed to serving for at least two more years on Cima's Representational Committee, which we consider to be one of the most critical and demanding committees. This committee plays a vital role in collating and reviewing personal requests submitted by citizens seeking public intervention to address various issues they have identified. All requests are reviewed with utmost care before being considered for inclusion in the committee's manifesto. It is worth noting that any requests deemed to be directly influenced by social media personalities are promptly rejected.

Every year, the citizens of Paeancea cast their votes on the contents of the manifesto, which includes requests that have been forwarded from higher levels of the governance structure. This reactive form of a referendum has proven to be a resounding success, as it empowers Paeanceans to take ownership of their world, free from the influence of political agendas. All proposals that receive a majority vote are then scrutinized by each governance committee, which assesses their relevance and conformity with the Constitution. As a testament to our commitment to transparency, all citizens are kept informed of the entire process.

Pan

Pan is the lifeblood of our civilization, the very foundation upon which our existence and prosperity depend. This highly sophisticated artificial intelligence is integral to almost every aspect of the functioning of Panacea. It oversees all machinery and production processes, from sourcing materials to delivering results, and manages the assignment of both human and robotic workers. Without Pan, I doubt that we could have thrived and sustained our way of life.

Pan is an indispensable facilitator of the entire governance process. It plays a crucial role in selecting candidates to fill positions within the governance structure, based on their qualifications and skills. While it is not directly involved in the decision-making processes of the governance committees, it provides invaluable support by streamlining decision-making procedures and assisting in their implementation.

Pan's involvement in our lives runs far deeper than many would expect, and I believe this is an area that would have horrified our ancestors. From the moment of our birth, we are all implanted with a microchip that connects us to Pan enabling it to monitor our health and safety and respond quickly in case of danger. Through this connection, Pan serves as a crucial conduit for our democratic participation by facilitating communication of our votes, suggestions, and comments.

During the initial rollout of Pan, many individuals expressed concerns about its omnipresence, particularly concerning its control over robots and cyborgs. However, these fears were assuaged when it became clear that Pan had been designed to prevent these machines from acting unilaterally by ensuring their compliance with its directives.

While some may worry that Pan's capabilities could be used to take over Paeancea, I defer to the expertise of those working on the technology and trust that Pan has been programmed to serve humanity and is incapable of seizing control. Although it exhibits some degree of sentience, such as awareness and empathy, Pan has been deliberately programmed to lack self-awareness, further mitigating any concerns about its potential for taking over.

Our lives

I would like to give you a glimpse into my family's experience since moving to Cima. During our formative years, my parents, sister, and I lived in a small apartment that lacked privacy and offered only basic and unappetizing food. This made it challenging for me, and I had to remind myself constantly of the reasons why we chose to move. Despite the difficulties, we spent quality time together as a family, engaging in creative pursuits like making short movies, inventing games and quizzes, and finding ways to entertain ourselves. Over time, our lives have improved significantly. My partner Samantha and I now derive a great deal of enjoyment from our lives, including good food, shared interests, hobbies, and friendships, all while continuing our studies.

My sister Cleo met her partner Jack and left the family home one year before Samantha and me. We were allocated an apartment that suited our demographics, in the same way as our parents were relocated to a smaller apartment.

Things continued to improve as more robots eased our daily labours, and new technologies continued to improve the quality of the food. We feel very fortunate when we recall the horrors that have encompassed our planet for the past century.

Cleo and Jack were the first in our family to produce the third generation of Paeanceans, with the birth of their son Alvid who was born in 2080. Samantha and I were next with the birth of our daughter Laetitia, born in 2083. Cleo and Jack went on to produce a second child, a daughter named Genny, who was born two years later.

From a young age, our children received a comprehensive education facilitated by our domestic robot, with input from Samantha and me. As parents, we were worried that they might miss out on developing essential interpersonal skills that we had learned during our childhood. However, the daily "social behavioural" classes they attended helped compensate for this concern. Our children received a well-rounded education that prepared them for success in both academic and social environments.

While performing our civil duties, we resided in the quarters provided by the Central Parliament of Cimas. These periods were far from unhappy or lonely; in fact, we relished the opportunity to meet new people and form meaningful connections with them. The work we engaged in was intellectually stimulating and rewarding. Through social interactions and involvement in various interest groups, we expanded our knowledge base, both in our respective fields of expertise and beyond. These experiences have had a significant impact on our personal and professional growth.

As second-generation Paeanceans, our education has expanded significantly beyond that of our parents. We have worked to reintroduce the lost sciences and incorporate them into our studies. Drawing upon our knowledge, we have developed educational courses for future generations and pursued innovative ideas to enhance the lives of our fellow Paeanceans. Our research is broad in scope, but strict controls govern the development and use of our inventions. Only those that directly support the well-being of our community and align with the production capabilities of Paeancea are adopted. All other concepts are documented and preserved for potential future use.

We take comfort in the knowledge that our children's futures are secure, thanks to the foundation established by our generation and that of our fathers. With this groundwork in place, we anticipate that a new world order will emerge, one that we hope will endure for generations to come. Nevertheless, we recognize that there are numerous challenges yet to be tackled, and we must pass the torch to the next generation to address them.

In the past 40 years, there have been several successful campaigns to encourage people to relocate to other cities. People apply to move for various reasons, most often it is their work that requires them to move closer to their colleagues or work location. For example, people working as environmentalists, geologists, or medical specialists, need to move closer to their area of work. Some people simply like the idea of a new life or joining their family members. Whatever the reason, it has several positive consequences. It increases genetic diversity, widens cultural understanding, and it helps to cement Paeancea as one global community formed by eight cities.

As members of my generation pass away or retire, we've witnessed tremendous progress in life expectancy. Advances in medical science and nutrition have led to an increase in the number of octogenarians and nonagenarians, with many even reaching their hundredth birthday. Despite some persistent health concerns such as cancer and neurological conditions, there has been a significant reduction in age-related illnesses. Moreover, thanks to epigenetic technology, we are making progress in removing inherited health risks from future generations. Nevertheless, for those of us who face incapacitation, euthanasia remains a viable option.

Our generation has made significant strides in preserving Earth's natural resources, helping ensure the continued survival of our species. Through a combination of sustainable practices and technological advancements, we have managed to minimize our impact on the planet. Although our contribution to Earth's ecosystems may be limited, we acknowledge that our relationship with the natural world is still parasitic, much like our ancestors before us. However, the key difference is that we have become more aware of the impact we have on our environment and are taking measures to minimize any harm we may cause. Rather than destroying the systems that sustain us, we strive to find ways to coexist with the natural world in a mutually beneficial manner.

The world is peaceful, I think we have reached the zenith of our Utopian ambitions. The eight cities of Paeancea live in harmony, there has never been a dispute that has led to any infractions, and there are no noticeable feelings of resentment or competitiveness between us. This ambitious project to save the human race which was conceived in the 21st century has been a resounding success.

There is a lot more that I could write about our lives, but I'll stop here and hand over the reins to the next generation.

Chapter Three

Third Generation

I am Laetitia, and the year is 2170. I am the daughter and only child of Henry and Samantha, both of whom, like my paternal grandparents, specialized in microbiology. I am 83 years old and widowed, having lived with my husband Joseph for 36 years before his untimely death. We have two children, Jarid and Helenap, and two grandchildren, Berwin and Freda. As was the tradition of his forefathers, Joseph kept a diary chronicling our lives in Cima. I will now use this diary to recount the story of our lives.

After reading the diaries of my predecessors, I find that there is little new that I can contribute to the management of Paeancea. The principles of governance, law and order, and the prevailing cultural attitudes have remained largely unchanged during my lifetime, echoing those of the early Paeanceans. Our current civilization model enables us to live sustainably within our environmental constraints, and thus, there has been little need for significant alterations except for some process improvements that improve our way of life.

While the primary focus of governance in Paeancea has been to improve the health and well-being of its citizens, equal emphasis is given to monitoring the path of natural recovery that restores the planet's ecological balance. We recognize the importance of preserving the planet's natural resources and ensure that our actions are aligned to maintain them for generations to come.

Our Wellbeing

Medical science has advanced by leaps and bounds over the years, leading to a significant increase in life expectancy. In the past 50 years, the average increase in life expectancy has been 9 months per decade. Today's younger generation can expect to live up to 100 years, with their physical and mental health maintained almost to the end of their life. People of my age are generally in good health and capable of making significant contributions to society. Unfortunately, my husband Joseph passed away nine years ago due to a neurological condition, which, at the time, was untreatable.

In recent years, there has been a decline in the number of women opting for natural childbirth, with the majority choosing to undergo cesarean procedures. There is currently ongoing research aimed at developing a laboratory procedure for embryo development, using donor eggs and sperm, as an alternative. This approach aims to eliminate the risks associated with traditional childbirth methods and reduce the likelihood of genetic defects through embryonic gene therapy.

The Natural World

Environmentalists have identified a growing imbalance in the planet's ecosystems, particularly in the area of biodiversity. Without natural predators, herbivore and rodent populations have exploded everywhere, destroying large swathes of flora. Although it is a natural process, it has put a lot of pressure on the rewilding of vast areas of the Earth.

Despite the principle of Paeancea that advocates for the natural evolution of global ecology, our generation has been working on reintroducing certain species of flora and fauna that have been lost over time. This has been made possible by the DNA banks left to us by our ancestors, with the hope of restoring the natural world to the rich biodiversity that existed before their extinction. However, it is important to note that it is highly unlikely that the natural world will be the same as it was 200 years ago.

The reintroduction of predators is helping to rebalance the ecology more quickly than would occur through natural evolution alone. However, finding an ecological niche that can support a reintroduced species has proven to be a significant challenge. In some cases, a complete ecological subsystem has been necessary to support the reintroduction.

Despite efforts to restore ecosystems, there are still areas of the planet that may take several generations, if at all, to recover. Extreme weather events are still common in certain regions, and phenomena such as fires, dust storms, and floods continue to cause damage to the environment. As a result, the Earth's landscape is vastly different from what it was for our forefathers, and it will continue to evolve in this new, changed state.

The loss of polar ice has had significant consequences, including rising ocean levels, changes to weather patterns, and altered weight distribution of water that has destabilized the Earth's rotation. While it is not the first time in the Earth's history that such changes have occurred, the long-term effects remain uncertain. Future generations must be aware of these ongoing environmental changes and their potential implications.

Social Evolution

The world we have inherited is largely peaceful and provides a happy fulfilling life for most of us. We no longer fear attacks from marauders now that most have died, and the few survivors who adopted an aboriginal lifestyle, do not at this time present a threat.

Living for decades in an enclosed world has created a strong feeling of social adhesion. This positive consequence has created a largely caring and harmonious society of people who nurture the objective of securing the future of Mankind, by building a cohesive global society that isn't destroying the fabric of its existence.

Today we have a lot more personal time now that robots have replaced most non-administrative functions. This has created a demand for new pleasure-seeking experiences such as the one that we have used, a tourist agency called Torisimo. This was created several decades ago to address this demand by offering organised trips to interesting places in all corners of the world.

I remember very vividly our first excursion. It came only a few weeks after we applied to visit the forests of Central Europe. This was before we had children, so the two of us took our seats in the transporter along with a dozen or more others. The flight took approximately ten minutes before landing in a hermetically sealed tourist encampment. This was still considered to be necessary, because even though there are fewer humans to transmit diseases, and the threats from infections have begun to disappear, the possibility of new pathogens in these remote locations, which could defeat our immunity systems, does remain a threat.

Our first morning was one that I have never forgotten. Even though this wasn't my first time outside of Cima, as an adult it now felt very strange, even frightening, as we left the security of the world we lived in. We were reassured that everyone experienced agoraphobia at first and that it would disappear over the coming few days.

As we left the encampment, a cacophony of noises, songbirds, grunts, roars, barks, and sounds from every direction. It was clear that the wilderness was thriving, meaning that the planet's ecosystems were recovering and that the sacrifices made by our forefathers had not been in vain. Our protective equipment could not distract us from this poignant moment.

The improvement in the quality and versatility of our meals enhanced our lives and changed our attitude towards nutrition from a primary necessity to a pleasure that we seek.

Whilst today the traditional family unit is still the norm, more and more people are looking to seek new experiences by choosing to cohabitate in other ways. Now you can find family groups consisting of three or more adults. My son Jarid has been in such a relationship throughout his adult life, which until now has not led to offspring.

Without the principle of a lifelong union, changing partners multiple times during a lifetime is not uncommon, leaving older children free to choose their guardians.

The use of recreational drugs is commonplace, especially among younger people who are seeking outlets for new experiences. Whilst the drugs are freely available and non-addictive, it is something that social scientists are concerned about. Escaping reality can become addictive, which some people believe may lead to a change in people's adhesion to society.

What Motivates Us

Reading back over the diaries of my ancestors, I see that they haven't mentioned how the absence of a monetary system has changed our attitudes towards materialism.

I know from our history studies that living within a monetary system was extremely different from what we now understand to be life's motivational forces. A world motivated by wealth and power brought success to millions but left billions in extreme poverty, and the failure of our forefathers to correct this gross imbalance contributed to the catastrophic events that brought about the near extinction of mankind.

My grandfather's stories about the early years in Cima revealed that survival was everyone's primary motivation. During that time, people focused solely on meeting their basic needs, and there was little expectation for anything beyond that. As a result, there was no need for a monetary system, and people simply did what they needed to do to survive.

Within my grandfather's lifetime, there was a gradual change of attitudes as people wanted more than basic needs and to add value to their lives.

Over the decades our lives have been enriched by the introduction of specialist interests such as archaeology, music studies, art history, gastronomy etc. In addition, more of the scientific disciplines that were lost during those early years have been reintroduced.

In recent years, a motivational system that some argue borders on a monetary system has been introduced. People receive E-vouchers for the hours that they work, regardless of the type of work. The vouchers have no intrinsic value other than to exchange them for such things as restaurants, hobbies, and vocational experiences. There is a ceiling set for the number of vouchers a person can possess at any one time and they cannot be transferred to anyone else. Special provisions are made for people who are unable to work for whatever reason. So far it has been a resounding success.

New Technologies

As mentioned in one of my predecessors' memoirs, there has been a moratorium on non-essential technological developments since the beginning of Paeancea. As a result, many of the sciences that existed before the creation of Paeancea have been lost, but thankfully the knowledge still exists in the vast digital warehouses.

Even though the introduction of frivolous technologies is still prohibited, in recent years the decision has been taken to reintroduce learning into new areas of chemistry, engineering, and physics. The first two reintroductions were not classified as frivolous technologies, and so quickly received the go-ahead.

The first was astronomy and all of the technologies that support it. Although the celestial telescopes and terrestrial observatories that had been created in the 21st century have long since ceased to function, the technologies used to recreate them are well documented.

The second to be reintroduced was space travel, specifically for the exploration of our solar system. There have been several debates in recent years about creating a mining facility on Mars to mine rare-earth metals and minerals; a lot of research was carried out by our ancestors, but unlike them, we will not seek to create a colony for the human race to escape to, there's no longer a need. Instead, the complete operation would be managed by robots.

The reintroduction of these old sciences has been well received, as they increase the subjects on the Higher Educational Studies syllabus, and gives people the opportunity to enrich their lives with self-improvement and personal achievement.

My Family

I would like to give you a glimpse of my daily life since I was a child, which has been typical of the lives of most Paeanceans.

My brother and I lived in the family home until we found our partners. As with all children then and now, we received our education from home, conducted by our assistant 'fifth generation' cyborg. The materials used for the studies came from the knowledge databases and the scientific materials that have accumulated since.

Apart from studying hard, we socialised with groups of adolescents around the same age, regularly getting together for social events and sporting activities, and sharing common interests that often took us to places in the world we had only read about.

I was ten when I took my first brief sojourn outside the confines of our city with three friends. It was an educational trip to an archaeological site, close to a city once known as Cairo. It was amazing, we were all excited as we viewed the unfamiliar landscape and the archaeological site, from the confines of the transporter.

We regularly joined other enthusiasts to participate in virtual study groups, my favourite being the discussions about art history. My mother, who has been studying it for several years, joined the group and gave us a lot of input.

Perhaps the most challenging and thrilling aspect of studying art history has been rebuilding the fragmented histories of global arts by researching and documenting them from thousands of data sources and then seeing them published.

After our children were born, Joseph and I continued with our studies, fitting them in with our research jobs at the Virology Laboratory. The formalisation of our partnership meant that we could apply for a spacious dwelling on the understanding that we planned to start a family. Our son Jarid came along shortly after we had settled into our apartment, and our daughter, Helenat, was born two years later.

As third-generation Paeanceans, we do not harbour the evangelical feelings of being the saviours of humanity, we never experienced the two generations of hardships and social evolution that brought us to where we are today. Our world functions without personal power and wealth, wars, nationalistic and racial prejudices, religion, farms, politics, disease and much more. This is completely normal, we have little idea of what any of it means.

Jacob's death came as a devastating blow to our family. He died from a massive stroke which took his life before anything could be done to save him. This was a shock as the health monitor should normally detect the warning signals that lead to a stroke. The postmortem showed that his monitoring system had malfunctioned and failed to detect the signs. The software of our microchips has been upgraded to prevent this from happening again.

I'm now living happily in a small apartment that is located in a complex which is specially designed to accommodate older people like myself.

A Look Into The Future

Amongst friends, we often discuss what we imagine is the future of Mankind. A change that is already occurring that will dramatically change things for future generations, is the process of moving people out of enclosed cities, into open areas. The city of Calama in the Andes is being relocated to a coastal area called Talama, located in what was once Peru. Pre-Apocalyptic, the once-remote town of Talama, was 80 km from the Pacific Ocean, but gradually became closer as sea levels rose.

The city is being constructed in a safe area and is not overtly impacted by climatic extremes, and importantly, has very little impact on the ecology. This ambitious re-siting project is designed to simulate the living conditions of the Pre-Apocalyptic period, with spacious houses, community centres and recreational facilities, connected by networks of transport hubs. This prototype development is being studied by the other cities, and based on the results, the remaining cities will be re-sited as soon as possible.

This as you can imagine will be a big step to take, but one that I'm certain will be welcomed by everyone, certainly me, even though it is happening a little too late for me to enjoy. The idea of returning mankind to something resembling the pre-apocalypse way of living has been a dream since the beginning of Paeancea.

While the immediate threats from marauders and pathogens have subsided, there remains a lingering fear that our society could inadvertently repeat the mistakes of our ancestors, leading to our eventual downfall. Nonetheless, the decision has been made to push forward with this next phase of social development. We recognize that our societal attitudes have evolved significantly from those of our predecessors, and the hope is that these attitudes are ingrained deeply enough within us to prevent a relapse into their destructive behaviours. While life is generally harmonious, human nature being what it is, we occasionally witness extreme emotional outbursts and criminal acts, though these are relatively rare occurrences. Access to weaponry is strictly prohibited, helping to maintain the overall safety and well-being of our community.

As humans, we coexist with the natural world, yet our existence exists parallel to it, without interfering with its evolutionary processes. We've developed methods for producing nutrition without harming life, generating energy without causing harm to the environment, and promoting physical evolution without relying on the natural selection of death and sickness. We're committed to limiting the production of dangerous chemicals and plastic that would otherwise pollute our planet. Our presence on Earth is no longer a threat to its continued existence, and we're dedicated to finding sustainable ways to coexist with nature for the benefit of all living beings.

Epilogue

I guess that this is the end of my family's memoirs since my children have not shown any interest in continuing it.

I can not predict the future of mankind, I just hope that we will be able to continue down our chosen path of Egalitarianism, that we can continue to believe in our community-led society and not drift into nihilistic beliefs, and that we can continue with one global community and not fall into the pit of separation and elitism.

In some perverse way, the near extinction was the saviour of mankind. It changed our thinking on how we should live within the framework of the world that supports us, changes that were unimaginable without the catastrophic events that threatened our extinction. It was as though humanity hit the reset button. I just hope future generations are not allowed to forget the horrors experienced by our forefathers.

When I read back over this hundred-year-old generational memoir I see that we have come a long way in such a short time. Certain environmental factors have shown a remarkable ability to recover, while others, especially climatic conditions, have remained unchanged or according to some scientists, have become increasingly violent. The balance of our ecology is so complex that it is not a given fact that it will ever return to pre-apocalypse levels.

Can we survive for another millennium? I believe we can.